Modern Combat Vehicles:3
LEOPARD

A.J.Barker

LONDON

IAN ALLAN LTD

First published 1981

ISBN 0 7110 1036 6

© A. J. Barker 1981

Published by Ian Allan Ltd, Shepperton, Surrey,
and printed by Ian Allan Printing Ltd at their works at
Coombelands in Runnymede, England.

The Canadians ordered 114 Leopard 1A3s
from the Germans – but before they did they
borrowed some 1A2 vehicles for training, seen
here on the ranges. *Canadian Armed Forces*

Contents

Acknowledgements

I wish to express my appreciation and
acknowledgement to those who have provided
the material from which this book is compiled.
In particular I wish to acknowledge the
assistance afforded by General a.D. Graf von
Schwerin, my old friend Generalmajor a.D. H.
J. Löser, and Krauss-Maffei AG and
Christopher F. Foss who has provided the
majority of the photographs, much technical
information and checked the captioning.

Cape Town   A. J. Barker

Introduction

The idea of the tank as a mobile, weapon-carrying, armoured platform is almost as old as warfare itself, and may be traced back at least to the Persian chariots which were equipped with revolving scythes to mow paths through the enemy ranks; for practical purposes however, the modern tank dates back to World War 1. In that war it soon became clear that improvements in the accuracy, rates of fire and killing power of small arms – the machine gun in particular – meant that infantry and cavalry could not break through fortified entrenchments without prohibitive casualties, and various attempts were made to break the stalemate deriving from this situation. The entrenchments could be devastated, barbed wire entanglements destroyed, and those defending the position stunned or killed by intense artillery bombard-ments – but such tactics meant not only that the element of surprise was lost but also that the ground was churned up and this created fresh obstacles to further advances. Furthermore both sides quickly realised that all they had to do to counter a systematic breakthrough was to reorganise their defences in depth, so limiting the attacker's gains. After 1917 the German infantry tried infiltrating tactics and these had some limited success. However as they were unable to cope with the logistic problems resulting from a sizeable breakthrough no worthwhile advance was possible. Only when the motor vehicle replaced the horse-drawn wagon as the mainstay of the supply services was a solution to the logistic problems possible, and in 1917 this solution was some 20 years away.

For the future the most significant development in the search for a means to break the deadlock on the Western Front was the revival of the concept of an armoured 'land ship'. Armoured boxes equipped with machine guns and propelled by internal combustion engines on self-laying tracks to give them cross-country mobility were devised; and in 1916 the first 'tanks' went into action on the Somme.* Achieving complete surprise they smashed through the German lines. But the new machines were heavy, cumbersome, mechanically unreliable and extremely uncomfortable. (They had no springs and when battened down for action their ventilation was such that the crews soon reached suffocation point.) Thus they were suited only to limited operations, and although they did manage to break through the German lines on practically every occasion they were used they never managed to penetrate to any depth; sooner or later the last of them would break down or run out of fuel and the Germans would bring up infantry reserves, counter-attack and seal off the gap punched in their defences.

On occasions individual tanks achieved minor successes which pointed the way to the future employment of such vehicles when their shortcomings had been overcome. On one such occasion a single British tank, after breaking through the German front, roamed around the enemy rear area shooting up supply columns, over-running static service installations, and generally creating panic. Ultimately its exploits came to an end when it overturned in a ditch.

The lessons of operations like this were not lost on a few far-sighted officers in both Britain and Germany. Lack of imagination stultified the majority however and between the wars tanks were envisaged essentially as a means of assisting infantry to dislodge an enemy entrenched in World War 1 type lines. In consequence most armies concentrated on designs of tanks intended as purely infantry support vehicles – slow, heavily armoured and generally equipped with little more than a machine gun as main armament. However the Germans – under the guidance of General Heinz Guderian and with Hitler's encouragement – followed a different line and seized on an important tactical innovation. Concentrating on fast medium tanks they created independent armoured divisions in which tanks were combined with motorised infantry. With the Luftwaffe providing the fire support in lieu of artillery, these Panzer divisions were expected to penetrate deep into the enemy's rear, disrupting and cutting his communications and isolating large forma-tions of enemy troops. It was a concept which facilitated Blitzkrieg and revolutionised armoured warfare, and it

---

* 'Tank' was originally a misleading British code-name, adapted for security reasons. In 1916 gigantic steel water cisterns were being constructed for British troops operating in the tropics, and few people were party to the secret that the word 'tank' referred not to those cisterns but to 'land ships'.

was vindicated in the early years of World War 2. Ranging far and wide over half Europe the Wehrmacht's tanks fought encirclement battles of staggering dimensions. In the first phases of the German invasion of the Soviet Union advances of up to 100km a day were common; in one battle alone 650,000 men were surrounded and taken prisoner. The tank, it seemed, was king of the battlefield and the role of the infantry had been reduced to that of a supporting arm. Even defence took on new mobile forms. The best answer to a tank, it seemed, was another tank; if possible one with a bigger gun and thicker armour. The result was a race towards even larger and heavier tanks, with bigger and bigger guns. Armour became many inches thick, and guns grew to the size of the 88mm of the German Tiger, and the 85mm of the Soviet T34.

With the end of the war in 1945 the race came to a temporary halt. Apart from those who believed that major wars were now a thing of the past, it was postulated that the tank had virtually lost its dominance to the atomic bomb. However the armour-gun race was reactivated when Soviet tanks in Korea confirmed the role of the tank in conventional operations. Moreover by this time the advent of the tactical nuclear weapon provided a new argument for armoured vehicles. Such vehicles, it was now suggested, could protect men from the effects of blast and nuclear radiation and enable them to cross contaminated ground quickly in order to close with the enemy. Those who took a different view pointed out that

new and formidable anti-tank weapons had been developed since World War 2. The argument still continues. However one of the best cases for the value of tanks in any future war was made by Marshal Malinovsky, a former commander of the Soviet Armoured Forces, when he wrote:

'. . . neither now, nor obviously in the future, are we able to dispense with the tank. The tank has many remarkable combat features which allow the successful execution of combat tasks in a nuclear war. Among all the other types of combat means, the tank alone is able to survive a nuclear burst, especially the shock wave and dangerous radiation. This is a very important attribute in modern conditions. In addition, the tank has high mobility, firepower and striking force . . . Many tasks still have to be executed by conventional firepower. Tanks are the best means for this. Thus, the tank-type combat vehicle will remain in service with our Army . . .'

The Arab-Israeli War of 1967 appeared to strengthen Malinovsky's contention just as events in the Arab-Israeli War of 1973 seemed to suggest that the future of the tank on a sophisticated battlefield may now be in doubt. The fact remains that the tank is a unique vehicle combining three basic factors – firepower, protection and manoeuvrability – into a single weapon system. However these factors are so interdependent that undue emphasis on any of them inevitably weakens the others. Many tank experts consider that high speed provides good protection for a tank trying to evade enemy fire. Moreover, with the possibility of tactical nuclear weapons being used on the battlefield, future armoured units need to be capable of high speeds and mobility – so that they can disperse over a wide area for safety and re-concentrate quickly for offensive operations. But there is a practical limit to high vehicle speeds over cross-country terrain and, although it is possible to design engines, transmissions and suspension systems for high speed performance, the resultant vehicle would lack combat potential, be extremely expensive to produce, and complicated to maintain.

Below: **Mobility of AFVs is not limited to their performance on the battlefield – they have to get there before they can fight. The size and weight of an AFV, therefore, limits its transportability, which could be crucial at time of war. Railways are still the most important method of transporting AFVs to the battlefield, although specialised tank transporters are used for shorter journeys. Here an Elefant (Faun SL T 50-2) tractor is seen with a Leopard on its semi-trailer. The Leopard is a 1A1A1 – a retrofit carried out to the Leopard 1A1, the most visible sign of which is the additional armour applied to the turret.** *Bundesministerium der Verteidigung (BdV)*

There is also a practical limit to the amount of armour that can be carried on a vehicle, and to the size and weight of the armament it carries. In short firepower and armoured protection are directly proportional to weight, and mobility is inversely proportional to weight. Consequently, in designing a tank a compromise has to be made. The minimum speed and performance required must be defined to determine the minimum permissible power-to-weight ratio, which will vary according to the size and type of engine used.

Railways are still the most important means of transport when moving armoured units over long distances, and railway transportation requirements – which differ from country to country – set a limit to the width of the tank. Furthermore with any tracked vehicle there is a certain range of values for the steering ratio (known as the L/C ratio) which is defined as:

$$\frac{\text{length of track on the ground}}{\text{width between track centres}}$$

If the L/C ratio is outside the given range of values then the tank simply will not steer. Thus the physical size of the tank is restricted, and with it the size of the engine and the associated fuel and cooling systems. (In practice it has been found that with conventional internal combustion engines the limit of engine power is 1,000hp. Leopard's engine develops 830hp and that of the British Chieftain 750hp.* But the power output of the engine determines the power-to-weight ratio, which in turn determines the weight of the vehicle. In effect therefore the power-to-weight ratio is dependent on what speed is considered necessary and this hinges on the question of mobility.

So far as a tank is concerned mobility primarily means cross-country movement and for this high power-to-weight ratios are important. Engine power is only one limiting factor in cross-country travel however. Equally important is the need for an effective suspension system to provide a smooth ride, the ability to be able to change gears smoothly and rapidly, and the ability to steer properly when the vehicle is moving across rough terrain. High speeds are possible only if hydro-pneumatic suspension systems, automatic or infinitely variable gearboxes and specially designed tracks are used. Sophisticated mechanisms of this kind invariably bring their own complications to the design as well as raising production costs. Nevertheless, in view of the probable future pattern of war in Europe, NATO tank designers now consider them worthwhile. (Seen from Moscow the likely course of events suggests there are other priorities. The Warsaw Pact armies pursue a doctrine of armoured

* The American XM1 uses a 1,500hp turbine engine; it is the first production MBT to use a turbine as its sole engine. The Swedish Strv103 has a turbine as an auxiliary engine.

*Left:*Russian T62s on exercise. This vehicle, armed with a 115mm main gun, epitomises the Soviet tank doctrines of cheapness, simplicity, mobility and reliability – over 40,000 are believed to have been built and it is used by many other countries. *Tass*

Above: The Bell AH-1S HueyCobra armed with TOW anti-tank missiles. The anti-tank helicopter has made the battlefield a much more dangerous place for the modern MBT. *Bell*

offence and to be sure of success they need large number of tanks – a minimum of three times as many as their opponents. Thus cheapness and simplicity are prime factors; so too is mechanical reliability and mobility.)

West German strategic experts view the situation somewhat differently to British and American strategists. All agree that conflict in Europe would probably start with an assault on West Germany by mechanised and armoured forces. For West Germany, therefore, the basic question is whether the Bundeswehr should give preference to a form of static or mobile defence. As mentioned earlier the possibility of nuclear weapons being used complicates the problem. But so long as the nuclear menace does not include the neutron bomb, the crew of a tank obviously has a better chance of surviving a nuclear strike than a detachment of infantry – even if the infantrymen are dug in. Because of its weight the tank can withstand blast; its armour offers protection against heat

waves and nuclear radiation; and if it is equipped with a pressurised air conditioning system no radioactive dust should be able to penetrate the interior. Furthermore if nuclear weapons are employed the tank will be able to move across contaminated terrain.

Whether or not the tank has a role on the nuclear battlefield is only one side of the coin. A whole range of effective anti-tank weapons has been developed since World War 2. Apart from long range guided missiles fired from the ground, such missiles have also been installed in helicopters, and from the 'tank busting' planes of 1944-45 a new generation of combat aircraft has emerged equipped with even more deadly anti-tank weapons. Other technical advances have also increased the tempo of conflict since infra-red sights and driverscopes will permit combat to continue even at night and radar has extended the limits of the battlefield.

It was against the background of the foregoing considerations that the West German Ministry of Defence began to examine the new German Army's tactical concepts and to draw up specifications for a new tank suited to these concepts.

In the event of a conflict the Bundeswehr experts concluded that NATO forces in the field would first have to slow up and delay the advance of enemy armoured columns into West German territory; because the attack would almost certainly involve an element of surprise and

be delivered by a force of overwhelming numerical superiority it was unlikely that the advance could be blocked or halted completely in the early stages. Loss of ground would have to be accepted and offset by time gained for the concentration and deployment of NATO's reserves. Apart from blunting the enemy's spearheads the aim would be to compel him to deploy for a set-piece battle as soon as possible. Following the delaying action there would be a series of defensive operations to contain the enemy columns and prevent any further advance and loss of territory. After that the final phase of the war would be offensive operations to drive the enemy back and destroy him.

Unfortunately the capabilities required for armour used in delaying, defensive and offensive operations differ. In delaying operations it is essential for the delaying forces to maintain contact with the enemy but equally essential that they avoid or evade any direct involvement. Disengagement demands good mobility and high cruising speeds, while perfect radio communications are needed to ensure the coordination of movement by individual units. Firepower is clearly most important, and to avoid direct involvement delaying actions are best fought at the furthest range possible. This should be the range at which the enemy is sighted, and the main problem here is a gunnery one – that of hit probability. Because the range is often limited by the terrain there is a further problem: in West Germany much of the countryside consists of rolling hills and woodlands – visibility is rarely more than 2,000m. Thus an enemy can not be seen and identified positively until he is within this range (although he may,

Above: **The Swedish Strv103B – better known as the S-tank – showing its turretless configuration. While the vehicle has a very low silhouette and weight, the problems of firing – especially on the move – are obvious! The vehicle in the photograph is equipped with a dozer blade folded under the tank nose and flotation screens. Note fuel tanks at rear of vehicle.** *Swedish Army*

Above right: **Leopard – the first Panzer built and designed by the Germans since World War 2. Tailor-made for its environment, it is amongst the most effective AFVs of its generation. The photograph is of a Leopard 1A4 showing its paces.**

in fact, have been detected beforehand).

Assuming a maximum combat range of 2,000m, the next question concerns armament. Should the tank be armed with a gun or guided missiles? As a trained tank gunner can fire six rounds within a minute at a target 2,000m away, while the rate of fire of the wire-guided anti-tank missiles in service with NATO armies in the late 1950s was only one round per minute, it appeared that the gun was superior to guided missiles at ranges of up to 2,000m.

This decision was reinforced when the question of ammunition was studied. There are three main types available to gun tanks: those which achieve their effect by piercing a hole in the armour, relying on their mass and velocity for penetration. Armour piercing discarding sabot (APDS) shells are included in this category of kinetic energy (KE) ammunition. A concomitant of penetrating power with APDS rounds is higher muzzle velocity which inevitably means increased barrel wear. The second type of ammunition, the High Explosive

8

Anti-Tank (HEAT) relies for its effect on the hollow charge or shaped charge principle. Unlike the KE round the effectiveness of the HEAT round is independent of its striking velocity so its muzzle velocity – and hence barrel wear – is lower. The third anti-tank projectile is known as HESH (High Explosive Squash Head). In this type of ammunition a large quantity of plastic HE is carried in a shell and it achieves its effect by way of shock waves which detach a 'scab' from the inner surface of the armour plate on the target.

The fact that all three types of ammunition can be fired from a gun, while guided missile rounds – because they are fin-stabilised in flight – are only suited to carry HEAT warheads, is a further argument in favour of arming a tank with a gun. Furthermore at ranges of 2,000m or less all three types of gun ammunition are more economical than missiles. Beyond 2,000m however the hit probability of a round fired from a gun tends to decrease.

The next question at issue was whether a tank designed for delaying actions should be rigidly mounted in a casemate (as is done in the Swedish Strv103 tank) or in a traversable turret.* For such operations there can be little doubt that only tanks with a traversable turret and gun stabilisation are capable of firing at the enemy while on the move in a withdrawal. Finally there was the overriding importance of mobility and manoeuvrability; and for this requirement the vehicle needed not only an adequate cross-country performance, but also a low

* Some details of the Strv103 are included in the section comparing the Leopard with other MBTs.

specific ground pressure if problems with the carrying capacity of bridges were to be avoided. Giving priority to these considerations meant, of course, restricting the weight of armour and, therefore, the ballistic protection it accords.

There were other problems for the Bundeswehr which related to their tactical decision. In defensive battles the purpose is to hold ground and the defending force stands to fight. Consequently the engagement is generally fought at shorter ranges than those prevailing in a delaying action. Firepower is therefore all important – especially if the enemy has numerical superiority; what is needed is a combination of high rate of fire and high hit probability. In offensive operations the situation is somewhat different. Firepower is still important, but mobility is of greater significance than in delaying actions. In any advance across Europe an armoured force taking the offensive will encounter water obstacles and as tanks are too heavy to swim they must be capable of fording such obstacles. They also have to be able to negotiate steep gradients such as river banks, and they need tracks which will grip well in muddy terrain and on icy roads.

It can be seen from the arguments put forward that the Bundeswehr's decisions for their main battle tank were related directly to the tactical situations foreseen to counter the threat of Soviet invasion. Leopard's final specifications were, therefore, a compromise between the mechanical and the tactical. The result was a tank tailor-made for its environment, a tank which people in the Federal Republic proudly refer to as the 'Panzer made in Germany'.

1. Development of the Leopard

In 1945 Germany was disarmed, her armament industry dismantled and its design teams dispersed. Thus in 1955 when the new German army of the Federal Republic was re-established, its equipment had to be provided from outside sources. The choice so far as tanks were concerned was strictly limited between the American M47 and the British Centurion. Economic, political and availability considerations weighted the choice in favour of the American vehicle and so by 1957 the Bundeswehr armoured units had been equipped with the M47 and an improved version of the same tank, the M48.

The American vehicles enabled the Germans to make a start on the training of tank crews, but it soon became clear that the M47 did not fit in with the tactical concepts which had emerged from bitter German experience gained in World War 2. Moreover the Germans saw an opportunity to rebuild their armaments industry and possibly even to enter the lucrative arms markets. In consequence it was decided to design a new 'Europanzer' in conjunction with the French and Italians who were in a similar position. The three nations agreed that production of the new tank should start in the mid-1960s and a common specification known as NATO FINABEL 3A5 was drawn up and issued jointly in November 1956. According to this specification mobility and firepower were to be given priority over ballistic protection; other important criteria were laid down in a document issued by the Technical Department of the German Ministry of Defence on 25 July 1957. These criteria called for:

● An all-up combat weight of 30 tonnes.
● A maximum height of 2.20m (7ft 3in) and width of 3.15m (10ft 4in).
● A power/weight ratio of 30ton.
● A radius of action of not less than 350km (220 miles).
● A gun capable of defeating 150mm (5.9in) of armour at 30°, with a maximum effective range of 2,500m (2,374yd) and two machine guns.
● An air-cooled multi-fuel engine and a torsion bar or air-hydraulic suspension system.
● A ground pressure of 0.85kg/sq cm (11.3lb/sq in).
In Germany two industrial consortia were formed to design and develop two competitive prototypes of the Europanzer, and the German Ministry of Defence

approved an order for four of these prototypes (two from each industrial group). In France the project was delegated to the Atelier de Construction d'Issy-les-Moulineaux, from whom the French DEFA (Direction des Etudes de Fabrication d'Armement, now Direction Technique des Armements Terrestres (DTAT), ordered two prototypes.

Firms which had already been striving to break into the world armaments market were among those participating in the German development. In 1955 Daimler-Benz had tendered for the supply of military vehicles to India, and had proposed that German industry might participate in the design, development and production of a main battle tank weighing some 36-39ton, specifically for the Indian Army. The firm F. Porsche KG of Stuttgart, better known for its sports cars, which was linked to this project, was to be responsible for the general design of the new tank and the manufacture of its chassis. Similarly Zahnradfabrik of Friedrichshafen was to be responsible for the transmission, Daimler-Benz for the engine, and Ruhrstahl AG for turret and armament. The hull of the new vehicle was to be fabricated by the Indian firm of TATA, India's Ministry of Defence was to provide the optical and telecommunications equipment, and the project visualised the production and assembly of 100 vehicles a year in one of India's state factories *(See specifications p107)*. Design and development, it was reckoned, would take four years and the first vehicles would start to roll off the production lines in the fifth year.

In due course Porsche produced a design for a 40ton vehicle, which was to be powered by a Daimler-Benz MB837A eight-cylinder diesel engine, manned by a crew of four, and armed with a 90mm gun. Both hull and turret were to be of cast iron, the former having 90mm of armour plate protection and 130mm maximum thickness on the turret. On the basis of these estimates it was calculated that the new tank would have a top speed of 50mph and that its effective weight would be in the order of 39,500kg.

In the event the project was abandoned at the design stage. However the fact that Porsche and others had done considerable work on it meant that German industry was in a favourable position to participate when the German

The re-establishment of the Army of the Federal Republic of Germany in 1955 led to the decision to equip with American M47s (above) and, later, M48s (right). The need to replace these vehicles in the 1960s and 70s led to the work on the Europanzer and, finally, Leopard. *BdV*

Left and below: **The Team B prototype.**
Krauss Maffei

Ministry of Defence called for tenders for the Europanzer.

Porsche led one of the two consortia and a group of designers from the firms of Porsche, Atlas-MaK of Kiel, Luther-Werke of Braunschweig and Jung-Lokomotivfabrik of Jungenthal constituted Team A. Team B – controlled by Ruhrstahl – consisted mainly of designers and engineers from Rheinstahl Hanomag and Henschel of Kassel. Italy, France and Germany had by this time agreed that mobility and firepower should take precedence over armour protection in the projected vehicle. This largely reflected the French view, although it was shared in large part by the Germans, and it was derived from the belief that the power of modern anti-tank weapons had outrun the defensive properties of armour. In consequence it was felt that safety should be sought primarily in speed and manoeuvrability. Shaped charge and high explosive anti-tank (HEAT) projectiles would be discounted, and the Europanzer's armour need only be sufficient to defeat conventional (KE) projectiles of up to 20mm, at the fighting range of the tank. However, great importance was attached to the necessity for another form of protection – protection against nuclear radiation and toxic agents ie against nuclear, biological and chemical (NBC) warfare. This implied careful planning of the fighting compartment together with the provision of some form of air-conditioning and aeration plant which would permit the crew to remain in action for a 24hr period without fear of their air space being polluted. To help make life bearable in such conditions it was proposed that the very latest human engineering techniques should be studied and employed where feasible. As to the question of fire hazard, it was considered that the use of a diesel engine would reduce this, but an automatic fire extinguishing equipment was to be built into the vehicle.

The two German teams completed their designs and produced wooden mockups in 1959 – within a year of their contracts being signed. Meantime Atelier de Construction d'Issy-les-Moulineaux, which was already achieving considerable success with its AMX-13, had concentrated French efforts into a single design, and their prototype was eventually designated the AMX-30.

In January 1961 Porsche's Team A presented two prototypes, designated A-1 and A-2 and eight months later Ruhrstahl's Team B offered its two prototypes, B-1 and B-2 *(See specifications p107).* A-1 was designated '723', A-2 '773', B-1 'TI' and B-2 'TII'.) All four prototypes incorporated a common turret developed by Rheinmetall and used the Daimler-Benz 838 engine. Additionally all four German vehicles were armed initially with a 90mm Rheinmetall gun. Apart from these common features however, the designs of the A prototypes were substantially different from those of the B prototypes. In the A models the suspension systems were of the torsion-bar type with seven road wheels, while the B models had air-hydraulic suspension and six road wheels. With both the A-1 model built by Jung-Jungenthal Lokomotivfabrik in Kirchen/ Sieg and the A-2 produced by a member of the Krupp Group, Maschinenbau of Kiel (MaK), the nominal

weight of the vehicle had risen to 35ton, largely because the turret originally estimated as 7.8ton had increased to 8.3ton. The two B models – presented by Rheinmetall-Hanomag of Hannover and Henschel of Kassel respectively – complied with the weight specifications but, after comparative trials at the Bundeswehr Proving Group near Trier in January 1961, prototypes A-1 and A-2 were judged to be superior. In simple terms the reason for this was that the A models were based on traditional concepts, were less expensive, and more suited to speedy production. By this time the 90mm gun had been replaced by a 105mm Rheinmetall weapon. (Subsequently two different 105mm guns were tried : the Rheinmetall and the British L7A1 which was later developed into the L7A3.)

In fact the trials at Trier were staged before the German contractors had completed their own tests, and this fact was reflected in the results. One engine failed during a 250km road test, an idling wheel jammed during a cross-country trial and various defects showed up in tyres and shock absorbers. But the fact that it had been agreed a trilateral commission would inspect the French prototypes in February (1961) and the German ones early in March set the date for the Trier trials. Furthermore, even if it had been possible to persuade the French to defer the work on the trilateral commission, arrangements had been made for the new tanks to be shown at the beginning of February to selected audiences of German politicians and senior officers, and to a panel of foreign tank experts. Another factor influencing the date of the Trier trials was that the French prototypes had already been put through their paces at Bourges, south of Orleans and in Satory near Versailles; from these they had emerged with a favourable report.

As the proving ground at Trier was not suited to firing trials comparative tests of the 105mm guns had to be conducted at a range in Meppen on the river Ems. From these trials and the earlier ones at Trier differences of view at both technical and political levels began to appear. Ultimately these led to the French deciding to produce their own tank (based on the AMX-30 equipped with a 105mm gun of French design rather than the British semi-automatic gun L7 for which the Germans had opted), although comparative tactical and technical trials were carried out between the German and French prototypes up to October 1963. Later, for political reasons the Italians also decided to back out of the Europanzer project, and to buy the US M60. This left the Germans on their own, with a growing need to replace their ageing M47s and no wish to buy the M60s.

These developments were of course in the future. So far as the Germans were concerned the trials of their four prototypes were completed by May 1962 and Team A was told to produce 26 copies of the A-2 model (now called the Porsche Standardpanzer). Team B received an order to produce six copies of prototype B-2; but only two of

these were actually assembled and the development of the B models was discontinued in the autumn of 1962.

The Standardpanzer copies of the A-2 prototype which eventually rolled off the assembly line incorporated a number of improvements and changes. Among these were increased armour protection and a greater vehicle width (3.52m – an increase of 100mm). Additionally the new vehicles had a somewhat better suspension system, improved transmission and a modified fire control system; the 600hp eight-cylinder engine used on the original tank was also replaced by an 830hp 10-cylinder motor. Based on the experience gained with the A-2 prototype the turret had been redesigned to allow the barrel of a 105mm L7 gun to be depressed to –9°. This entailed cutting back some of the barrel support which, in turn, altered the position of the centre of gravity, with attendant problems. Minor changes were also made to the turret basket and the gun control equipment.

By this time the Germans had decided to adopt the Vickers L7 gun, designed and built in Britain, and which in 1960 was the most advanced tank gun in existence. So during the autumn of 1962 1,500 guns of the current L7A3 model were purchased to equip the Standardpanzer and the tanks which would follow when they were mass produced. And, as the L7A3 had been specifically designed for the British Centurion MBT and the US M60, the decision was an important step towards standardising tank ammunition within NATO.*

Testing of the new prototypes started at Meppen in late 1961 and it was soon found that the transmission was not suited to the more powerful 830hp engine. The first step was to replace the coupling between engine and transmission but the problem was not overcome until improved lubrication and a better cooling system were installed. The results of the various tests also showed that the chassis would have to be improved, and modifications were made to the steering gear, the braking system, hatches, air cleaners, engine air intake and fuel system, fighting compartment, heating, cooling and aeration system. (The latter was especially important because of the specified NBC requirement.)

Tests of the new turrets started in March 1962 and were conducted concurrently with the engineering and running trials; their purpose was to determine how the turret components would behave while a tank was being driven at high speed over rough terrain. The L7 gun and its related sighting system were also tried out at the same time to see how their components would stand up to simulated battle conditions. In the end it was concluded that neither the turret, the gun nor the optical equipment

* The German decision to adopt the L7 ended Rheinmetall's programme to produce a gun capable of firing a spin-stabilised hollow-charge missile developed in France. It is relevant to add that the French did not adopt the L7 and continued to develop their own gun.

were yet fit for mass production, and before they could be classed as such most of the components needed considerable modification. The gun mounting, for example, had not stood up to the stresses imposed on it during the high speed cross-country tests and had to be redesigned. So too had the recoil and recuperator mechanism since it was found that firing three different types of ammunition (APDS, HEAT and HESH)* with their varying muzzle velocities produced target patterns which showed considerable deviation. It also became apparent that the machine gun which had been installed for ranging purposes was useless for this purpose since it was effective up to only about 1,800m, while accurate ranging – because of the gun's flat trajectory – was not necessary until after about 1,500m. To overcome this a rangefinder was clearly necessary. But none capable of determining ranges up to 2,500m was available, and as

* The Leopard actually carries five types of ammunition: APDS, HEAT, HESH, HEP and smoke.

Left and below left: **Leopard second series prototype: note lack of rangefinder and the mount for the ranging machine gun (RMG) in the mantlet. The RMG was replaced by an optical rangefinder because the former was found to limit the range of the 105mm main gun.** *Krauss Maffei*

Below: **Pre-production Leopards showing exhaust louvres' differences. Note lack of optical rangefinder; all these vehicles have ranging machine guns.** *Krauss Maffei*

the tank commander's and gunner's telescopes could not do so either a new optical rangefinder had to be developed. In the event this was done in record time by the firm of C. Zeiss of Oberkochen, and it was installed for use by the tank commander. Unfortunately, however, its installation necessitated a further modification to the turret which had to be raised.

During September 1962 six out of the total of 17 Standardpanzers which were then available were handed over to the Bundeswehr's 93rd Panzer Training Battalion in Munsterlager for troop trials. Before these trials were completed in March 1963 the German Federal Armaments and Material Office sanctioned the manufacture and assembly of 50 pre-production tanks incorporating the modifications recommended during the trials. Delivery of these pre-production vehicles, code-tagged by Porsche 'Model 814', started early in 1963. (17 were manufactured by Jung-Jungenthal, another 17 by Luther and Jordan of Braunschweig, and the remaining 16 by Maschinenbau GmbH of Kiel.) Meantime the intensive activities at Meppen were continuing. Arduous test runs were made in mud and sand and on steep slopes and in all of them the Standardpanzer behaved impeccably. In the ditch crossing, fording, and submerged trials which followed they were equally successful. By means of a snorkel mounted on the tank commander's hatch a Standardpanzer was capable of submerging to a depth of 5.3m, and during both deep fording tests – up to the turret roof line – and in the submerged trials it proved possible to shut off the engine and re-start it after a 10min interval.

Cold weather trials were conducted during the winter

months of 1962-63 at the Munsingen proving ground in Swabia. The object of these tests was to ascertain the behaviour of the vehicles at low temperatures and in snow and ice. Their results were assessed as satisfactory, revealing much useful information which was subsequently put to good use in developing tracks with a high cohesive power.

In October 1962 comparative trials were staged with a Standardpanzer competing against the French prototype AMX-30. Observers from the US, the Netherlands, and Belgium attended these trials, which focused on a 250km road test and a five-hour cross-country run – each to be completed without any breakdown and in the shortest possible time. The results favoured the Standardpanzer which attained an average cruising speed of 60.8km/hr in the road test, while the French prototype vehicle achieved an average speed of only 50km/hr. Similarly in the cross-country runs the Standardpanzer was equally successful, completing the tests without breakdown and at average speeds of 24km/hr. The minor faults which did show up during these trials were easily corrected, and the modifications fed back to be embodied in the design of the pre-production and production models.

Despite the superior performance of the Standardpanzer compared with the French prototype the foregoing trials were not considered definitive, however, and in September 1963 a fresh series of exhaustive technical and tactical comparative trials were carried out between Standardpanzers and French tanks (which had by this time been officially designated AMX-30). So far as the Germans were concerned the die was cast in as much as during the July preceding the new trials the German Defence Committee had decided to mass produce their improved version of the Standardpanzer and equip the Bundeswehr with it. But the trials went ahead, directed by an evaluation committee composed entirely of Italians, watched by French and German experts and attended by observers from Belgium and the Netherlands.

The tactical trials started on 16 September 1963 at Mailly-le-Camp, the French Proving Ground in Champagne Province, with five German and five French tanks participating. The first test was a 300km run and all 10 tanks took part. One French and one German tank failed to finish the course because of engine failure, and the German tank had to be withdrawn from the competition because a crane was needed to remove and replace the powerpack, and the rules of the competition did not permit this. The next trial was a gruelling two-day performance test under simulated battle conditions, and at the end of it both French and German tanks were judged to be about equal. Comparative engineering trials followed, with the AMX-30 being tested at Bourges and Satory while the German vehicles were tested at Meppen. In effect these particular trials were virtually a repetition of those of October 1962, except that a 100km test – half of which had to be run with petrol and diesel respectively –

replaced the earlier 250km road run. (On 1 October the Standardpanzer had been redesignated Leopard and it was under their new name that the German vehicles operated from now on.*) Both German and French tanks were again judged to have performed equally in this road run.

The results of the remaining tests were much the same; it seemed that there was little to choose between the Leopard and the AMX-30. However it did appear that despite its greater combat weight (40ton as against the AMX-30's 36ton) the Leopard had a better cross-country performance than the French tank, could move just as fast on roads (about 10% quicker in fact) and had 18% better acceleration. Because the French gun fired only a spin-stabilised shaped-charge projectile while the L7 British gun in the Leopard fired three types of ammunition no valid comparison of the main armaments of the two tanks was deemed possible. In any event the French were not prepared to accept the conclusions of the Italian evaluation team – to the effect that the Leopard was marginally superior to their AMX. And as changes in France's defence posture meant that no money would be available for the purchase of tanks until 1965 at the earliest, the French decided to opt out of the joint development of the Europanzer and to press on with the development of their own AMX-30. For their part the Germans were now set on replacing the Bundeswehr's ageing M47s with the Leopard, and DM150,000million were allocated for this purpose in the Defence Budget of 1964. In due course this was to lead to the firm of Krauss-Maffei AG of Munich being charged with setting up an assembly line and organising the preparations for the production of 1,500 Leopards – an order that was subsequently increased to 1,800.

Meantime development of the pre-production models was continuing. An intensive study was made of the fire control system – the optical equipment in particular. And by 1964 approximately 7,300 rounds of ammunition had been fired from the guns of seven of the vehicles participating in the tests, and 8,000 rounds of machine gun ammunition. Simultaneously six other Leopards were tested and tried on road and cross-country runs, in ditch crossing operations, and on steep gradients. (All in all these six vehicles covered some 68,600–49,600km on roads and 19,000km cross-country.) And in July 1964 there was an underwater test. Near the road bridge at

* For the past 40 years German armoured fighting vehicles have been named after ferocious wild animals – such as tiger, panther, grizzly bear etc.

Left: **In 1967-68 the Dutch Army tested the Leopard 1 and Chieftain. They eventually ordered 453 Leopards which were delivered 1969-71. This vehicle shows the Dutch stowage box modification on hull sides but has not yet been fitted with smoke dischargers, of which the Dutch have their own variety.** *Dutch Army*

Rodenkirchen three Leopards fitted with snorkels successfully crossed and recrossed the Rhine – which is 4m deep and 320m wide in this area. While they were submerged control of the Leopards was exercised by radio signals picked up by an aerial mounted on the snorkel. On surfacing all three tanks fired their main armament and machine guns, to demonstrate they were unaffected by their submergence.

When France opted out of the development of a Europanzer, Italy – the third partner in the trilateral arrangement – was in a difficult position. Like the Bundeswehr the Italian Army was equipped with the obsolete M47 which had to be replaced, and the Leopard was one of the possibilities the Italian considered. Thus it was that between May and July 1964 two of the pre-production Standardpanzers were put through yet another set of proving trials at the Italian Armoured Corps Training Centre at Cape Teulada on the southern coast of Sardinia. Initially these trials were conducted by teams of Italian and German experts, but when the Italians had collected sufficient results for their evaluation, the German team prolonged the trials in order to gather more data regarding the behaviour of the Leopard during driving and firing at high temperatures over extremely difficult terrain. These tests showed conclusively that the optical equipment, the gun and machine guns, the suspension, the power train and the cooling system were capable of standing up to high temperatures. Furthermore the dust clouds raised by the vehicles travelling at about 40km/hr on the road tests demonstrated the efficiency of the crew and engine compartment ventilation systems.

In April 1965 another two of the Standardpanzers were tested at the Belgian Armoured Warfare School at Leopoldsbourg by the Belgian Army, and in January 1966 two pre-production Leopards were sent to Britain in exchange for two Chieftains for comparative trials in both countries. Meantime a series of cold weather and snow trials had been mounted at Camp Shilo in Canada; these ran from December 1965 until February 1966. Then in October 1966 the Norwegian Army began a series of evaluation trials at Trandum and Snoeheim in Norway, which lasted a year. Finally, between December 1967 and May 1968 the Dutch Army also tested two Leopards and two Chieftains at their Armoured School in Amersfoort. From all these trials the Leopard emerged with flying colours, resulting in Norway, the Netherlands, Belgium and subsequently Italy deciding to equip their armies with the Leopard.

But this was not the end of the story. In June 1974 Denmark also decided to equip her army with Leopards and ordered 120. Then, after comparative trials between the Leopard and the American M60A1, Australia ordered 90 of the latest mark of Leopard – the 1A3 for delivery between 1977 and 1981. And during June 1976 Canada decided to buy 114 Leopard 1A3s, fitted with Belgian computerised fire control systems and laser rangefinders, for delivery in 1978. Greece finally ordered 106 MBTs and four ARVs to be produced between Feb 1983 and Apr 1984 by Krauss Maffei (73) and MaK (43 plus ARVs) with an option for a further 110MBTs. Turkey has ordered 81 MBTs and four ARVs (54 by Krauss Maffei, 27 by MaK). Italy has talked about a new order for a further 160 'specialised versions' of the Leopard 1. Since the time of writing 225 of the Bundeswehr's 420 Gepards have been fitted with laser rangefinders.

2. Production of the Leopard

As mentioned earlier the design and development of the 26 prototypes of the Leopard was undertaken by a group of designers from various firms. To mass produce the new tank, however, the German Ministry of Defence decided to utilise another group of firms and to appoint a general contractor who would coordinate production and be responsible for quality control of the components and sub-assemblies provided by the subcontractors, assembly of the vehicles, their final testing and their maintenance after delivery. Four different firms or groups of firms tendered for this 'management' contract, and in the summer of 1963 the German Ministry of Defence announced that it had been awarded to Krauss-Maffei of Munich – a well-known engineering company with over a century's experience in building railway locomotives.

Wegmann and Co of Kassel, an armaments firm which produced turrets for the Tiger tank during World War 2 and which had developed the turrets for the protoytpe Leopards, was given the contract for producing the turrets needed for the series production of the new vehicle. Rheinmetall GmbH of Dusseldorf, another firm having long association with the armaments industry, was to be responsible for the gun systems and minor assemblies in the turrets. Motoren- und Turbinen-Union (MTU) of Friedrichshafen was to produce the engine designed for the Leopard by Daimler-Benz, and Zahnradfabrik Friedrichshafen AG, also of Friedrichshafen, would manufacture the transmission system. Over and above these firms manufacturing the major components, about 2,700 other companies are currently involved in the Leopard project, manufacturing and assembling parts. For example Blohm and Voss AG of Hamburg, a well-known ship-building firm, produces the tank's hulls. Similarly the huge electrical engineering corporation of Allgemeine Elektrizitäts-Gesellschaft AEG-Telefunken of Frankfurt supplies the infra-red night sights and the combined infra-red/white light searchlight with which the Leopard is equipped. (A brief review of the other main firms involved in the manufacture of Leopard and its associated vehicles is contained in Appendix 2.)

Two years elapsed between the signing of the contracts and the first series production Leopard rolling off the assembly line. For Krauss-Maffei they were two years of feverish activity. Before production could start the activities of all the 2,700 odd firms participating in the project had to be coordinated, an assembly line set up, techniques devised to monitor production at various stages and special tools developed and manufactured, technical manuals compiled. In the event the first Leopard to be completed left the assembly line on 9 September 1965 and was officially 'taken over' at a ceremony attended by Germany's Minister of Defence.

To ensure a smooth flow, the assembly line is composed of 17 individual assembly stations connected by a roller conveyor. Each station has a pre-assembly

Below: **Leopard 1 production line at Munich.** *Krauss Maffei*

19

area, and the flow from them is controlled in accordance with the output determined for any given day; some of them are used exclusively by Krauss-Maffei's inspection department. Delivery of components and parts is linked to the output rate and each component and part is subjected to inspection before it is embodied in the next stage of production. For example the hulls – coming from Blohm and Voss AG – are subjected to careful dimensional checks before they are moved to the assembly line. (This despite the fact that they have already been checked in Hamburg.) Similarly the powerplant (engine, cooling system and gear box – all of which are made by different firms) are tested separately before they are assembled at a separate subsidiary powerplant assembly line. Then, in its assembled form, the complete powerplant is tested to see if it functions properly before it is moved to the assembly line proper.

The turret is mounted on the hull and the tracks fitted at the two last stations. The engine is then started up and after a brief final check-out the completed Leopard is

driven away under its own power to a test track for a series of trial runs, which include tests on steep slopes and submergence. During the trials the tank's performance and that of its components are closely monitored and any faults that become apparent are corrected. The radio system is also installed and tested in this last phase of production. Finally the vehicle is turned over to an independent team of inspectors of the Bundeswehr.

By the end of 1965 about 600 Leopards had been produced, and the German Army had already taken over about 100; 50 more were now coming off Krauss-Maffei's assembly line every month. Reference has already been made to the Belgians and Norwegians and Dutch deciding to re-equip their armies with Leopards; the Belgians placed an order for 334 Leopards in December 1967 – of which the first was delivered two months later; Norway ordered 78 in November 1968; the Netherlands followed with a contract to buy 415 in the following month and subsequently increased the order to 468. Then, following evaluation trials in September 1969, the Italians arranged to buy 200 Leopards from Germany in addition to producing 600 others under licence. These were manufactured by a consortium of firms including Fiat, Breda and Lancia and directed by OTO Melara of La Spezia. Production in Italy was to have begun in 1972 and completed in 1974 but the first Leopard 1A2 (which was the version ultimately built in Italy) only

Left: **Leopard 1A4 turrets being fitted with 105mm guns at Rheinmetall's Dusseldorf facility.** *Rheinmetall*

Below: **Leopards ARVs and Marder MICVs (right) in production at Krupp MaK at Kiel.** *Krupp MaK*

rolled off the assembly line in September 1974 and the order – since increased from 600 to 720 – is still in production.

In the event the Italians took delivery of their first Leopards in the spring 1970; these were produced in Germany and destined to become 'demonstration' tanks at the Italian Armoured Corps School at Caserta. The balance of the 200 ordered from Germany followed and by early 1973 the three armoured regiments of the Pozzuolo del Friuli Brigade had received their full quota of Leopards.

Denmark in June 1974 ordered 120 of the latest model of Leopard – at that time the 1A3 with deliveries to begin in 1976. They were delivered between March 1978 and November 1978. Australia followed up with an order for 90 Leopard 1A3s – they were delivered between 1976-78 and were fitted with the Belgian SABCA fire control system. Canada too decided in June 1976 to buy 114 Leopard 1A3s. Finally there have been the orders from Turkey (150 of the 1A3 version, 40 of which had been delivered by the end of 1977) and the interest expressed by Greece in producing the Leopard under licence.

Meanwhile back in Germany the Bundeswehr had increased their demands from the initial 1,500 to 2,187 in 1972 and to 2,437 in 1974. In sum this meant that by the end of 1976 firm orders had been placed for 4,561 Leopards, of which 4,171 had actually been produced.

NOTE ON THE DISPOSAL OF THE LEOPARDS WHICH ARE NOW IN SERVICE:
West Germany
In 1978 the Government of the German Federal Republic announced that it was reorganising the Bundeswehr, and

Right: **Leopard 1s of the Belgian Army. Note replacement of the usual MG3 on the turret by a FN 7.62mm MAG weapon.** *Stephen Tunbridge*

Below: **Italian Leopard 1A2 produced in Italy by OTO Melara of La Spezia. The Italians expect to produce 600-800 Leopards.** *OTO Melara*

that the German Army will eventually have 16 Panzer brigades, of three tank battalions each and 20 Panzergrenadier brigades with two tank battalions each. Each tank battalion will have three companies with 10 tanks each (each company having three platoons of three tanks at battalion HQ – giving a total of 33 tanks per battalion).

Italy
In the Italian Army the Leopard tank regiments have 45 tanks – 10 in each of four squadrons and five with the regimental HQ.

Belgium
The Belgian armoured regiments to which Leopards have been assigned are organised into independent squadrons or squadron groups, each of three squadrons with 17 tanks per squadron.

The Netherlands
Like the Belgians, the Dutch have assigned their Leopards to 17-tank squadrons (each of three platoons with five tanks apiece and two with the squadron HQ). In

lieu of the MG3 machine gun, the Dutch have mounted Belgian-made MAG machine guns on their Leopards, Dutch smoke dischargers in banks of six and optical sights to use the British L52 APDS round.

Norway
Norway's 78 Leopards have been issued to the tank regiment in the Northern Brigade, and to one battalion of the Southern Brigade.

Australia
The 90 Leopards purchased by Australia have been used to equip a single Leopard battalion.

Canada
Most of the 114 Leopards, called the C1 by the Canadians, bought by Canada will be issued to the 4th Canadian Mechanised Brigade Group, which is currently assigned to NATO.

3. Characteristics of the Leopard 1

The Leopard has a crew of four – commander, driver, loader and gunner, and in common with most other battle tanks the driver sits in the front part of the hull while the other three members of the crew are located in the turret. The latter rotates through 360° and houses the main armament and the two machine guns as well as the crew. On the assumption that in battle the crew be confined to their vehicle for prolonged periods of time the vehicle has been designed and fitted out in such a way as to make life as comfortable as possible. Apart from conventional features such as padded seats and an electric heater to cook food and prepare hot drinks, the Leopard's air conditioning, ventilation and heating systems make life inside the tank considerably more bearable than is generally the case is most fighting vehicles. To make engine starting easier in cold weather conditions the exhaust heat of the heating system can be used to preheat the coolant in the radiator and air from the heated crew compartment can be blown over the batteries to warm them. In hot weather the heating system's fresh air blower can be used as a fan. But, to anyone who has travelled in a Leopard the outstanding sensation is one of an incredibly smooth and *quiet* ride even when moving fast over rough ground. The main reason for this may be attributed to the torsion bar suspension system which uses seven roadwheels on each side with wide roadwheel travel. This wide travel allied with five hydraulic shock absorbers reduces pitch and roll vibrations even at high speeds over

Below: **Early production Leopard 1 – note verticals on exhaust louvres at rear of hull.** *Krauss Maffei*

Right: **Detail of commander's hatch on the Leopard 1A4 with telescope guard on left of photograph.**

Below right: **Detail of loader's hatch showing MG3 mount and periscopes.**

Below: **The main armament of the Leopard 1 is the British-made L7A3 105mm gun. This drawing shows the in-turret components: 1 gun barrel; 2 gun cradle and shield; 3 recoil guard; 4 main gun empty cartridge bag; 5 scavenging system; 6 empty cartridge bag for coaxial 7.62mm machine gun; 7 coaxial machine gun with electrical firing mechanism.** *Krauss Maffei*

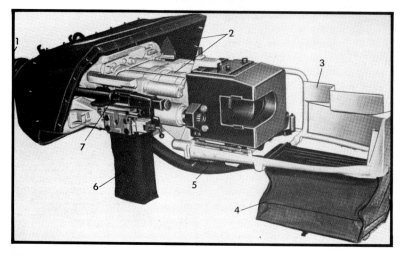

Right: **Closeup of the MG3 7.62mm machine gun and four smoke dischargers. The photograph also shows clearly the spaced armour retrofitted to Leopard 1A1s to bring them to 1A1A1 standard.**
Michael Ledford

cross-country terrain, and makes for crew comfort and a stable gun platform.

The first Leopards (designated Leopard 1) were equipped with the 105mm high-performance gun; this was designed and built in Britain although the German versions were fitted with improved breech and recoil mechanisms. (The decision to equip NATO tanks with guns of 105mm was taken after a NATO study which concluded that the prospective combat ranges in Central Europe would be about 2,000m. The 105mm gun is accurate and effective well beyond this range.) The gun consists of a rifled tube with 28 grooves and, to prevent toxic fumes getting into the crew compartment, a bore evacuator is fitted in the middle of the tube. The bore evacuator is a hollow sleeve around the gun tube. When a round is fired some of the propellant gases enter the evacuator through gas ports in the tube. As soon as the shell leaves the muzzle of the gun the gas collected in the evacuator flows rapidly back through these ports, dragging the propellant gases in the rear half of the tube forward and out of the muzzle. The breech mechanism is semi-automatic, having a horizontal sliding breech block which opens automatically after a round has been fired and then closes automatically when a new round has been loaded. This makes for a high rate of fire – in the order of 9-10round/min. As a further measure to prevent fumes from residual gases in the spent cases fouling the crew compartment when the breech of the gun is opened, the spent cases are collected in a bag which is fitted to an extractor/scavenging system.

The gun can be layed either manually or by an electro-hydraulic drive system, and an override control enables the tank commander to take over the gunner's functions of sighting, laying and firing. Elevation range is between –9° and +20°. The weapon itself has demonstrated remarkable accuracy with tests showing that the L7A3 gun firing APDS ammunition can put 99 rounds out of 100 into a tank turret target measuring 0.80m by 1.50m at a 1,000m, achieve a 100% hit rate firing at a tank size target at the same distance, 98% rate at 2,000m and an 89% rate at 3,000m.

The ammunition racks are located in both turret and hull, within easy reach of the loader : 60 rounds are carried, 19 of which are in the turret, the other 41 in a rack on the left of the driver. The Leopard carries three different types of armour-piercing ammunition – APDS, HEAT, HESH and smoke. Because of its flat trajectory and high velocity the APDS projectiles are accurate and effective even at long range : the shaped charge HEAT rounds are capable of defeating the armour of any tank currently in service; while the HESH projectiles are multi-purpose rounds for use against both hard and soft targets.

The Leopard's secondary armament comprises two 7.62mm MG3 machine guns with 5,500 rounds of ammunition, 1,000 of which are carried in the turret. One of the machine guns is mounted coaxially to the left of the main gun; the second can be mounted on the turret roof beside either the commander's or loader's hatch for anti-aircraft defence. The MG3 is an improved version of

Left: **The MTU MB838 CaM500 diesel engine as installed in Leopard 1.** *MTU*

Below: **Details of main components of the Belgian SABCA fire control system which is installed in Leopard 1s of the Australian, Canadian and Belgian armies.** *SABCA*

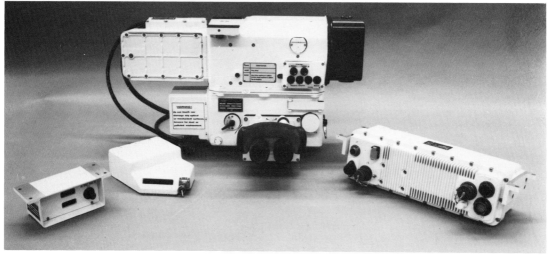

the famous MG42 with a cyclic rate of fire of 12round/min. Like its predecessor which made an enviable name for itself with both the Wehrmacht and the Allies in World War 2, the MG3 is a most reliable weapon, well able to resist dirt and rough treatment. The coaxial gun is equipped with an electrical firing mechanism and follows the laying movements of the main armament. If the need arises however both machine guns can be dismounted and used in a ground role.

There are also two sets of four 76mm smoke dischargers. Firing them either in a single volley or in two volleys of four produces an 80m wide smokescreen at a distance of approximately 60m from the tank. This particular type of smoke grenade launcher has been in service with the Bundeswehr for some considerable time and is regarded as completely reliable.

The Leopard's fire control system is an elaborate one. Fourteen periscopes are provided, eight for the commander, three for the driver, two for the loader and one for the gunner; this makes for good all round vision even when the hatches are closed. A variable power (x6-x20 magnification) panoramic zoom telescope is mounted on the turret roof in front of the commander's hatch, and even in poor light the commander can observe the terrain and range targets. A flexible shaft connecting the telescope and azimuth indicator enables the target to be tracked while the turret is being tranversed. For night fighting the panoramic telescope can be replaced by an infra-red sighting device which operates in conjunction with an infra-red searchlight; this searchlight can also project white light. For the gunner there is a binocular rangefinder and a coaxial monocular telescope. The

MTU diesel from above right front and above left behind.
(Front) 1 Fuel pumps; 2 Crank case intake; 3 Heater plugs; 4 Oil
reservoir; 5 Fuel filter; 6 Supercharger. (Rear) 1 Water manifold; 2
Supercharger manifold; 3 Injector pumps; 4 Fuel injector; 5
Exhaust; 6 Heat exchanger; 7 Oil filter; 8 Oil filler;
9 Dipstick.

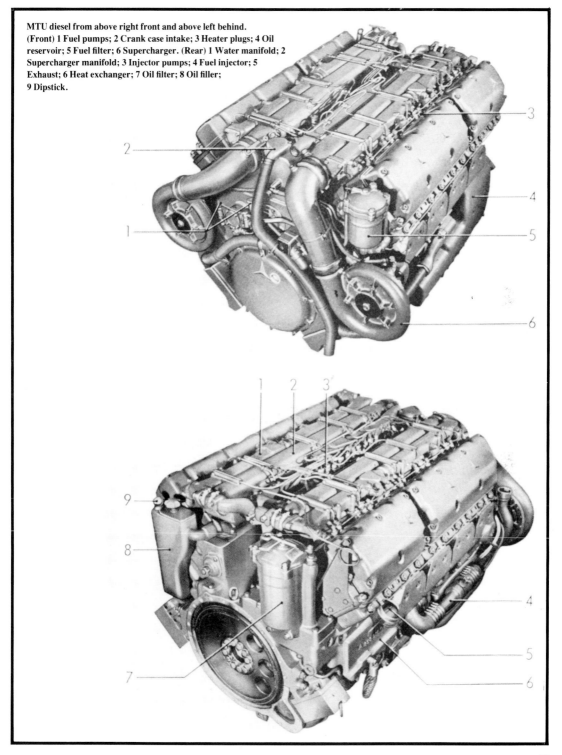

rangefinder, which can be used for both stereoscopic and coincidence ranging, doubles as a sighting device. All three optical sighting devices are fitted with automatic flash shutters which close the sights for a quarter of a second when the gun is fired so that the muzzle flash does not blind the crew.

The engine and transmission of the Leopard are at the rear. The engine is a 37.4litre 10-cylinder 90° V-type supercharged diesel capable of running on either diesel fuel (F-54) or jet fuel (F-40). Based on a 1960 Daimler-Benz design it is not only powerful but compact also – enabling a complete automotive unit to be replaced in about 20min with the help of the Leopard armoured recovery vehicle. The motor is liquid cooled, and has a dry-sump lubrication system which assures the oil being circulated even when the vehicle is inclined at an acute angle. At 2,200rev/min it develops an output of 830hp which gives the vehicle a road speed of 65km/h(40mph). Fuel capacity of 985litre(217 Imp gal) and a consumption (of diesel) on roads of 165litre/100km gives the Leopard a range of some 600km (375 miles).

The Leopard's transmission has four forward and two reverse speeds and is equipped with a hydraulic torque convertor, electro-hydraulic gear changing and a bypass clutch – a combination which enables the driver to change gear rapidly and easily even when moving over difficult terrain. Speed, mobility and manoeuvrability provide good additional protection for a tank, and in the Leopard this is achieved by providing two gear shift positions for forward travel : 'forward cross-country' and 'forward'. In the 'forward cross-country' position the torque converter is connected in the first three gears – depending on the vehicle's speed; consequently the driver can overcome small obstacles without having to shift and so does not run the risk of stalling the engine at a critical moment. In the 'forward' position however, the torque converter is switched on in the first gear only, the clutch being operated when the other gears are shifted. This increases the efficiency of the transmission and effects a marked saving in fuel.

The Leopard is steered by a two-radii cross-drive steering transmission. This, together with the shift transmission, fan drive and summation gears, is installed in a common housing and actuated mechanically and hydraulically. The large steering radius is designed for high speeds on roads, and if the driver turns the steering handle beyond a pressure point of the large radius, the small gear-dependent fixed radius is brought into action and this gives the vehicle tremendous manoeuvrability, especially on cross-country terrain. It is hoped that these radii – which are relatively small for such a heavy vehicle – might enable the Leopard to evade a guided missile; certainly by using its steering differential the tank can twist and turn almost within its own length with great rapidity. The steering handle, which looks like a horizontal figure 8, is located in the right front portion of the hull; the tank can also be driven from a secondary driving position in the upper part of the turret and this is customarily used when the vehicle is fording a water obstacle.

For night driving the driver has an infra-red 'driverscope'. Infra-red filters are mounted on the vehicle's headlights and the driverscope replaces the middle of the driver's three periscopes. The commander can also replace his front periscope with a second infra-red driverscope and so help the driver to negotiate difficult terrain.

Mention has been made earlier of the Leopard's torsion bar suspension system, which is rugged, simple and extremely effective. The system consists of seven rubber-tyred light alloy road wheels on each side, mounted on road arms connected to individual torsion bars which run transversely across the hull. Between road wheels one and two, two and three, four and five, six and seven there are four small diameter support rollers. The first three of these and the last two road wheels have hydraulic shock absorbers and there are buffer springs to serve as bump stops and to limit the torsion angles of the torsion bars.

The tracks themselves are high alloy steel connected by double pins, rubber-bushed, and fitted according to the circumstances either with 55cm wide slide-in rubber track pads or steel anti-skid combat tracks with a ground contact of 4.23m (13ft 11in). There are also special spiked track pads for use in snow. Changing from one set of tracks to another takes approximately two hours.

The electrical system operates at 24V on eight batteries located in the fighting compartment, and is charged by a three-phase generator. The whole system is controlled by a master switch on the driver's instrument panel, and the electrics in the turret are connected to the main power supply by way of a slip ring. All the cables are water and dustproof, detachable and easily replaced.

The hull of the Leopard is fabricated from steel armour plates welded together, while the turret is cast in one piece; the suspension is protected by lateral skirting plates. Although the characteristics and thickness of the armour plate and the armour steel of the hull remain classified, it is estimated that the armour on the front of the hull is about 70mm thick and that of the turret about 52mm thick. This will not afford the same degree of protection as the armour of the heavier British Chieftain, but within the constrictions of the specifications laid down the German designers accepted they could not hope to achieve complete immunity against armour piercing, shaped charge, and squash-head projectiles. They elected to give priority to firepower and mobility (unlike Britain, the United States and the Soviet Union whose current tanks all emphasise firepower and ballistic protection over mobility). However the Leopard has a low silhouette and its curved surfaces increase the likelihood of projectiles ricocheting off hull and turret. Furthermore

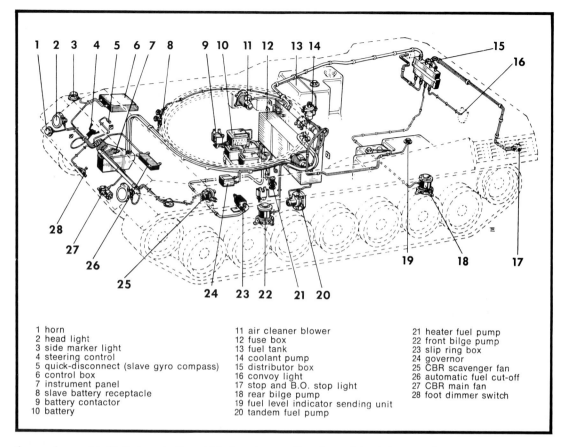

1 horn	11 air cleaner blower	21 heater fuel pump
2 head light	12 fuse box	22 front bilge pump
3 side marker light	13 fuel tank	23 slip ring box
4 steering control	14 coolant pump	24 governor
5 quick-disconnect (slave gyro compass)	15 distributor box	25 CBR scavenger fan
6 control box	16 convoy light	26 automatic fuel cut-off
7 instrument panel	17 stop and B.O. stop light	27 CBR main fan
8 slave battery receptacle	18 rear bilge pump	28 foot dimmer switch
9 battery contactor	19 fuel level indicator sending unit	
10 battery	20 tandem fuel pump	

the openings and ballistic traps in the vehicle have been reduced to a minimum, and the designers maintain that the Leopard comes very close to the optimum ballistic configuration of a main battle tank.

A special camouflage paint protects the Leopard against detection by infra-red sighting devices at night, and protection against heat detection is provided by mixing the exhaust gases with air and so reducing their temperature.

Besides affording protection against missiles and projectiles the armour of today's fighting vehicles has a secondary role. It must be able to protect the crew from the effects of nuclear radiation and the flash, heat and blast effects of a nuclear explosion. Armour plate is well suited to this task – although it must be added that nothing can be expected to protect tanks close to ground zero. The blast wave from a powerful explosion quickly degenerates with distance and initial radioactive radiation is only effective up to a point where the blast wave will cause heavy damage. Thermal radiation may scorch the outside of the vehicle some way beyond this point, and even set paint and rubber components on fire – but the crew inside a Leopard should be safe. They will also be

Above: **Leopard electrical system.**

protected from radioactive dust collecting on the outside of the vehicle, since the Leopard is virtually hermetically sealed and its ventilation and air conditioning systems can be adjusted to create a pressurised crew compartment supplied with filtered air. This means that on a nuclear battlefield the Leopard would be able to cross safely a stretch of radioactive ground or pass through a radioactive dust cloud. Vehicles doing so would have to be decontaminated of course, but the Leopard is easy to decontaminate and the filters in the air conditioning system are simple to exchange – although they are in fact designed to withstand several successive sorties through radioactive dust at concentrations which it is believed are unlikely to occur.

At this point mention must be made of the techniques used when the Leopard has to cross a water obstacle. Prior to such an operation all the chassis openings on the tank are closed hydraulically – the muzzles of the guns are sealed, the rangefinder is covered by flaps operated from inside the tank and if the water is deep a snorkel is mounted. This is a large diameter telescopic collapsible

Above: **Leopard 1 equipped for deep fording during an exercise on the River Moselle near Trier.** *Krauss Maffei*

ventilation tube carried in a bracket on the outside of the tank. It is in three sections so can be adapted to the depth of the water. From the snorkel – which in effect raises the height of the commander's hatch – the commander controls the vehicle through the crew's intercom. The preparations for such an operation take about 10min, and the vehicle is able to cross watercourses up to 4m deep. During the crossing the air to the engine is taken in through the snorkel and passes to it via the crew compartment. Spring loaded valves on the exhaust are switched on and off by a submergence hydraulic system, allowing the exhaust gases to flow directly into the water. To dissipate heat while submerged the cooling system is flooded, but a thermostat control protects the engine from undue cooling. Any water that has got into the vehicle is sucked out by two electric bilge pumps, one for the engine and the other for the crew compartment. As soon as the obstacle has been crossed, the Leopard is ready to go into battle almost immediately. All that has to be done is to discard the snorkel and traverse the turret through a few

degrees to dislodge the plugs on the coaxial MG3; the muzzle cap on the main gun is penetrated as soon as a round is fired and the flaps covering the chassis are opened merely by reducing the pressure in the hydraulic system which controls them.

An efficient fire extinguishing system has been built into the Leopard as a protection against attacks by napalm and other incendiary mixtures as well as the flash of a nuclear explosion. Fire extinguishing foam is piped from two containers through nozzles which operate automatically when the system is triggered by warning sensors at temperatures of 175°C. First the foam is sprayed over the entire compartment; if that is not sufficient the driver has two other extinguishers which can be operated manually.

Radio communications are provided by an SEM25 radio system composed of two sets. There is also an intercom system for the crew and an external telephone enabling the infantry to talk to a Leopard and vice versa. The two radio sets are frequency modulated transceivers with a frequency range of 26-69.96MHz. A total of 880 channels are available for communications, 10 of which can be pre-set and changed quickly by means of a rotary switch. Each transceiver is connected to its own 2.5m whip antenna and a special antenna tuning unit.

4. Versions and Variants of the Leopard 1

Current Models

The first production versions of the Leopard were designated simply *Leopard*. In 1968 however – by which time nearly 3,000 Leopards had been completed – a variety of improvements were introduced and the tanks which incorporated them were designated *Leopard A2*, the older ones being designated *Leopard 1*. In 1971 it was decided to modify all the old Leopards (Leopard 1 of the first four production batches) issued to the Bundeswehr, and the modified tanks were redesignated *Leopard 1A1*. Then, in 1974, 232 Leopards built in Germany during the previous two years (the fifth production batch), and the version of the Leopard built under licence in Italy which all incorporated the same modifications as the 1A1, were designated *Leopard 1A2*. In effect it is virtually impossible to distinguish between a Leopard 1A1 and a Leopard 1A2.

Leopard 1A3, produced in 1973-74, was a development of the Leopard 1A2; and *Leopard 1A4*, the latest version in service, is based on the 1A3 but incorporates still more improvements.

(For specifications of Leopard 1 see p108.)

Leopard 1A1 (ex-Leopard, ex-Leopard 1) and Leopard 1A2 (ex-Leopard A2)

The improvements which led to the eventual designation Leopard 1A2 included the fitting of a new stabilisation system to the main armament. This system, produced in Germany at Mainz by Feinmechanische Werke and known as WSA1, reduces the time the tank has to remain at rest while firing and enables both the target and the shot fall to be observed while on the move. With it the Leopard is said to have a 50% first-round hit probability, firing at a target range of 1,400m while travelling at a speed of 15-28km/h (9-17 mph). With the better observation it confers, the new stabilisation system makes for improved fire support and hence economy in the use of tanks in a fire support role. Because it enables a firing position to be taken up more rapidly, it reduces the tank's vulnerability. The original electro-hydraulic laying system did not have to be modified when the stabiliser was installed.

Other improvements introduced into the Leopard 1A1

Below: **Early production Leopard 1.** *Krauss Maffei*

33

Above: **Early production Leopard 1. Note early pattern engine exhaust louvres, stowage of equipment on hull sides, stowage basket at turret rear with box for infra-red searchlight when not in use.** *Krauss Maffei*

Below: **Leopard 1 (fourth production batch).** *Krauss Maffei*

included a light alloy thermal sleeve fitted to the main armament. This sleeve is similar to those fitted to the guns carried by the AMX-30 and British Chieftain, and its purpose is to lessen any distortion of the barrel caused by uneven cooling after firing due to atmospheric conditions – wind, rain or ice, etc – affecting only one side of the barrel.

New tracks with flexible rubber pads which are ideal for both road and cross-country travel were also fitted to the Leopard 1A1. For operations in deep snow or on ice the pad at every eighth or ninth link can be replaced by a special spiked crampon. At the same time mudguards and

Three views of the Leopard 1A1.
Note the eccentric fume extractor
on the 105mm gun and the lack of a
thermal sleeve for the barrel.
Krauss Maffei

This page and above right: **Four views of the Leopard 1A2. All these vehicles have thermal sleeves on their 105mm main guns and rubber side skirts. The vehicle in photograph at left has a wading attachment over the commander's position. Note the differences between the Leopard 1A2's cast turret and the welded turret of the Leopard 1A3 (below right).**
All Krauss Maffei

heavy steel-reinforced rubber skirts were fixed to the sides of the vehicle to shield the suspension system. These skirts, besides reducing the amount of dust, water or snow thrown up by the vehicle, protect the suspension against hollow charge projectiles.

The Leopard 1A2 differs from the Leopard 1A1 in only minor respects. The Leopard 1A2 has a stronger turret, better filters in the ventilation system and the infra-red equipment used by the commander and driver in the earlier Leopards was replaced by light amplification periscopes. A spotlight with an infra-red filter has also replaced the left front headlamp. Among other minor improvements in the Leopard 1A2 which deserve mention was new fording apparatus which included lifejackets for the crew, and a longer tow cable than was issued to the Leopard 1A1. The latter had turned out to be too short, especially when tanks disabled during a fording or wading operation had to be pulled out of the ditch. The final improvement was the incorporation of an automatic device preventing the commander's hatch being opened if the pressure inside the crew compartment were at a level which would endanger the crew while the tank was wading through water.

Leopard 1A1A1

Leopard 1A1s have been retrofitted with spaced armour to the turret and mantlet and have become Leopard 1A1A1s. This modification has not been made to any Leopard 1A2s.

Leopard 1A3 (ex-Leopard A3)

Leopard 1A3 incorporated all the improvements of the Leopard 1A2 together with others. Among these the most noticeable is a completely new welded turret made from spaced armour; this replaces the old cast turret. The space between the armour plates is filled with a special material and it is claimed that this reduces the effect of the hollow charge ammunition still further. The turret in the Leopard

Left and overleaf, below right and left: **Three views of the Leopard 1A3.** *Krauss Maffei*

37

Above: Leopard 1A2 (without skirts, left) compared to the 1A3.
Krauss Maffei

1A3 is about 1.5cu.m bigger than that of its predecessors, making the crew compartment more comfortable. 110 of the 1A3 version were produced for the Bundeswehr in 1973-74, 120 for Denmark and 42 for Australia.

Leopard 1A4 (ex-Leopard A4)

Based on the 1A3 the Leopard 1A4 has the same turret but with a marginally higher commander's cupola. In addition it includes a new (COBELDA) fire control system based on an electronic computer (the earlier versions of the Leopard had a stereoscopic rangefinder which served as the gunner's sight), and a daylight infra-red panoramic telescope for the commander. 250 of the Leopard 1A4 have been produced since 1974, and in 1975 it was proposed to produce another 250 but the Bundeswehr did not confirm the order and it lapsed.

As a result of all the improvements the combat weight of the Leopard has risen from 40,000kg (Leopard) to 41,500kg (1A1), 42,500kg (1A2 and 1A3). Nevertheless until they are replaced by another generation of tanks the Leopards now in service will probably continue to be modified to incorporate further improvements. One such modification currently being effected is the fitting of all Leopards with the completely new (GWS-2HR-A) automatic gear selector developed by Zahnradfabrik Friedrichshafen AG.

Optional Leopard 1 Equipment

Krauss Maffei offer a number of modification kits for the Leopard 1 which include a number of items – stowage boxes on hull side, SABCA fire control system – already

Below and right: **Head on views of Leopard 1A4. The ribbing on glacis plate is to hold snow/ice grousers, visible on photograph at right.** *Krauss Maffei*

adopted by other countries (Holland and Belgium respectively). Other modifications are: additional armour for turret (cf Leopard 1A1A1), stowage of all ammunition below turret ring (which reduces dramatically turret fire risks), armoured side skirts, automatic transmission, the stowage box and fire control system alterations mentioned, dozer blade (Australia has adopted this), new gunner's sight, new snorkel, passive searchlight, passive commander's and driver's periscopes, a tropical kit and a stabilisation system for the main gun.

Projected developments

In 1975 a consortium of firms – Blohm and Voss, MaK Machinenbau GmbH of Kiel, and Ingenieurburo Dr Hopp – suggested that a more powerful version of Leopard 1 could be developed by replacing the L7 gun with a 120mm smoothbore weapon, and by fitting a new engine and heavier armour. This tank – to be known as the 'Improved' Leopard or Leopard 1A5 – was offered to the Iranian Government of the Shah which at the time of its demise was considering buying 1,000 of them.

In 1975 also another consortium of German and Italian firms (Krauss-Maffei, Dr Hopp, Blohm & Voss, Diehl KG Remscheid, Arnold Jung, MaK Maschinenbau GmbH, Luther-Werke of Braunschweig, OTO Melara, Fiat and Lancia) was formed whose aim was to produce in

Italy a cheaper version of the Leopard 1. The hull, engine, transmission and armament were to be the same as those of the Leopard 1, and so too would the electrical and optical systems – with the exception of the electro-hydraulic stabilisation system fitted to the main gun; the latter would be replaced by a less expensive Swiss system. But the turret would be different, being constructed from angled welded steel plates. Initially this version of the Leopard was designated the Leopardino,

Four views of the Leopard 1A4. *Krauss Maffei (2); BdV; Krupp MaK*

though the name was subsequently changed to Leone (Lion), and the intention was to market it to Middle East and Third World countries. The German firms in the consortium would produce approximately 50% of the components, including hull, engine and transmission, while the Italians produced the remaining 50% – including the turret, the armament and electrical equipment; the Italian firm of OTO Melara would also be responsible for assembling the vehicles at La Spezia. The first prototype was to be completed in 1977 and it was hoped that the Leone would go into series production in late 1978. (In the event the tank did not attract the attention that was hoped for.)

Above and right: **Two views of the Leopard 1A1A1 – the updated and uparmoured version of the Leopard 1 and 1A1 – showing clearly the additional mantlet armour and the side and rear turret armour which covers the stowage baskets. Both vehicles have thermal sleeves on their 105mm main guns and early exhaust louvres.** *Wegmann*

44

5. Derivatives of the Leopard 1

To sustain the efficiency of modern tanks on the battlefield specialised support vehicles are needed. Ideally such vehicles should have similar characteristics in terms of speed, mobility and protection to the tanks they are supporting. Ideally also, to ease production, maintenance and training problems, both tanks and support vehicles should be constructed from the same components. Plans for a 'family' of support vehicles based on the Leopard started early in the development phase and led eventually to the series production of armoured recovery, armoured engineer and bridgelaying vehicles. An anti-aircraft tank, the *Gepard* (Hunting Leopard), has also gone into production, and there have been studies in the design of a self-propelled 155mm gun/howitzer, using the Leopard chassis. The turret for this gun/howitzer has been developed in France for mounting on an AMX-30 hull, and as the original Europanzer specification stipulated turret rings for both AMX-30 and Leopard, the Germans had no problem

Above and left: **A private venture between Krauss Maffei and GIAT of France involved the marrying of a Leopard chassis with a French 155mm GCT turret. (A specification for this project can be found on p110.)** *Krauss Maffei*

mounting a French 155mm gun/howitzer turret on a Leopard in 1973. But the Bundeswehr is committed to the development of a 155mm self-propelled gun in a joint programme with Britain, and interest in the Leopard SP gun project appears to have waned.

Armoured Recovery Vehicle (Bergepanzer Leopard)
(For specification see p109)

The role of armoured recovery vehicles is the recovery or repair of tanks which have broken down or been disabled on the battlefield. In World War 2 many disabled tanks had to be abandoned because of a lack of suitable recovery vehicles, a lesson the Germans remembered. In consequence, studies on the design of an armoured recovery vehicle started while the Leopard was at the prototype stage. The Bundeswehr's experience with the American armoured recovery vehicle then in service with the German Army – the M74 and M88 – was put to good use by Porsche's design team, and the chassis of the new Bergepanzer was created from proven components of the

Leopard 1. Only the recovery and lifting equipment had to be developed, built and tested. Prototypes were produced by the firm of Jung-Jungenthal in September 1966 and in due course the vehicle went into series production under the auspices of MaK Maschinenbau GmbH of Kiel. The suspension, tracks and powerpack (including the cooling and exhaust system) are identical with those of the Leopard 1. So too are the ventilation and heating systems, NBC protection, driver's seat, commander's hatch, tool kit and most of the other equipment carried in the vehicle; the fuel system is almost identical.

The crew is four – commander, driver and two recovery mechanics – and the ARV can cruise at speeds up to 65km/h, with a range of 800km. It can cross water obstacles with a depth of about 2m without any auxiliary equipment, and with the Leopard snorkel kit it can undertake submerged operations to a depth of 4m.

The most striking feature of the vehicle is its traversable jib-boom which can be used to lift

Left: **Leopard ARV recovering a waterlogged Leopard 1. Note use of dozer blade by ARV as a brace.** *Krupp MaK*

Below left: **Another view of a Leopard 1 recovery by an ARV.** *Krauss Maffei*

Right: **Rear view of the product improved Leopard 1 ARV, 100 of which have been delivered to the German Army. This version of the ARV has a hydraulic jack mounted at right rear and a more powerful crane.** *Krupp MaK*

components up to 20tonne (19.7ton) in weight; this can include a complete turret or a powerpack. A hydraulically operated dozer blade at the front of the vehicle is used either for clearance work or as an earth anchor for heavy pulls or lifts. Used as a dozer the vehicle van move up to 200cu m/h, and with additional side attachments the width of the blade can be extended to 3.75m. If required it can be fitted with four scarifiers to rip up the surface of roads.

The ARV has two winches. The main one, a tow winch with a horizontal cable drum, is mounted in the centre of the operating compartment; the cable itself has a diameter of 33mm and a length of 90m. In a straight pull it can move 35tonne (34.5ton) and up to 70tonne (69ton) if a guide pulley is used. A hydraulically driven cable tensioning device automatically extends or rewinds the cable. The second winch, a hoisting winch with a vertical cable drum, is mounted on the right hand side of the crew compartment. To ensure that the cable is properly wound when it is retracted there are guiding grooves on the drum and, when the cable is wound off, three turns remain on the drum to maintain friction when the cable is under tension.

Finally, over and above the standard tools for motor vehicle servicing and maintenance – such as lifting jacks, tools to mount and tension tracks and pumps, to fill and drain fuel tanks – the vehicle carries a very wide range of special tools to enable the crew of four to carry out a multiplicity of repairs in the field. This special equipment includes electric welding and cutting equipment which will work from the ARV's power supply; a mechanical chain saw, together with a bracket and lifting tackle to enable a complete Leopard powerpack to be carried on the deck of the vehicle.

Armaments comprise one machine gun mounted in the forward section of the hull and a second on an anti-aircraft mounting above the commander's hatch. There is also a smoke grenade launcher mounted on the left of the

vehicle consisting of two sets of three projectors which are fired electrically. The radio which has a range of 25km and communication equipment are similar to that in the Leopard.

The German Army has already taken delivery of 444 of the original Bergepanzers and a further 100 of the improved version, which has an increased lifting capacity and is fitted with a stabilising jack at the rear of the hull. Six of the original model have been supplied to Australia, 36 to Belgium, eight to Canada, 69 to Italy, 52 to the Netherlands and six to Norway.

Armoured Engineer Vehicle (Pionierpanzer Leopard)
(For specifications see p109)
The armoured engineer vehicle, first produced in 1968 and manufactured by MaK Maschinenbau of Kiel, was designed to meet the requirements of NATO armoured engineer units and it can carry out a wide range of engineer tasks. It was developed from the armoured recovery vehicle, which externally it closely resembles. However, in place of the spare powerpack on the rear deck of the recovery vehicle, the Pionierpanzer carries a large earth-auger; it also has a ladder mounted on the jib-boom. The auger can be used to excavate foxholes, and 30 such holes – 0.7m diameter and 1.9m deep – can be drilled in an hour.

One other important difference between the Bergepanzer and the Pionierpanzer is that the latter has been fitted with a modified dozer blade so that the vehicle can undertake intensive and continuous bulldozing activities. A heat exchanger has been installed in the hydraulic system to enable this to be used at high ambient temperatures. As with the Bergepanzer the dozer blade is mounted on the nose of the vehicle and is actuated by two hydraulic cylinders through two lever arms. When the vehicle moves back four scarifiers mounted on the blade tear up the soil which is then bulldozed away when the vehicle moves forward.

47

Left: **AEV showing clearly the stowage of the auger in place of the spare powerpack which can be carried by the ARV.** *Krauss Maffei*

Below: **Leopard Pioneerpanzer (AEV) using its auger.** *Krauss Maffei*

Right: **Leopard AEV crossing an AVLB (armoured vehicle launched bridge.) Note that the ladder on the jib-boom has been removed.** *BdV*

Below right: **Leopard Pioneerpanzer using its dozer blade.** *Krupp MaK*

Large storage compartments permit the transport of a considerable quantity of explosives for demolition purposes. Engineer tools and equipment are also carried as well as the specialist equipment which is a feature of the recovery vehicle. Like the Bergepanzer the Pionierpanzer has a deep fording capability and using a snorkel it can cross water obstacles to a depth of 4m.

There have been 36 Pionierpanzer Leopards built for the German Army, 14 for the Netherlands, 12 for Italy and six for Belgium.

One current development which deserves mention is a new combat engineer vehicle for the German Army; its purpose will be to prepare river crossing points. Two firms – Maschinenbau GmbH of Kiel (MaK) and Eisenwerke Kaiserslautern (EWK) Goppner – are involved, and prototype vehicles of what will be known as the 'GPM' (Gepanzerte Pioniermaschine) have been built based on the chassis of the Leopard 1 tank. The prototypes of both firms have a dozer blade at the front, but the MaK model has a single hydraulically operated excavator while the EWK prototype has two such excavators. Following comparative trials the EWK prototype has been selected for series production – with one minor change, that the production vehicles of the future GPM will be based on the chassis of the Leopard 2.

Left: **Two more views of the Pioneerpanzer deploying its auger. Note equipment stowage on hull sides.** *BdV*

Right: **One of the two prototype German combat engineer vehicles, the EWK GPM, seen in action using its hydraulically extending excavator arms to push itself backwards up a bank. Also clearly visible is the in-line arrangement of the crew positions. The second prototype by MaK has only one excavator arm. Based on the Leopard 1 chassis, if production commences the Leopard 2 chassis will be used.**

Below: **Front view of the Pioneerpanzer with dozer blade in operation. Note scarifiers under the blade and the bow machine gun at right of hull front.** *Krauss Maffei*

Armoured Bridgelayer (Bruckenlegepanzer Leopard)
(For specification see p109)

Bridgelaying equipment speeds up the crossing of obstacles such as narrow rivers and ravines. The German Army's armoured bridgelayer is the *Biber* (Beaver); it is based on the Leopard 1 chassis, and uses a virtually standard Leopard hull less the turret. Both the bridge and method of laying it are unique. Previous bridgelayers have always used 'fold-out' types of bridges, either an 'up-and-over' or a scissors. But both present a large target, visible for considerable distances when the bridge is being launched. Biber is different, since its bridge is carried in two symmetrical halves and extended horizontally. Thus it is less likely to reveal the site of the bridgelaying operation and the element of surprise may be retained.

Two prototypes using different methods of horizontal bridgelaying were built and compared. The first was a telescopic projection system relying on an extendable telescope on which the bridge was rolled forward; once the bridge was across the obstacle the telescope was retracted. The second system developed by the firm of Klockner-Humboldt-Deutz extended the bridge as a cantilever, with the tank chassis counterbalancing its weight. It was this cantilever system which was selected and put into production by MaK Maschinenbau GmbH.

The bridge itself is made of a light metal alloy, and in the retracted position it is 11.65m long. Even when the bridge is being projected the overall height is never more than 4m (dramatically less than the Chieftain AVLB's 12.2m). In the travelling position the two symmetrical halves rest on the chassis, the upper section (track) and the lower section being connected by web plates. Struts between the track carriers are mounted in such a way that the bridge remains flexible in its longitudinal axis in order to compensate for different cant in the two support ends of the bridge. (The bridge can be established even if there is a considerable difference in elevation at the two ends – as much as 5m down and 2.5m up.)

Before the bridge is projected the two sections are jointed together and the Biber pushes out a dozer blade at the front end of the vehicle to brace its front end. The front section of the bridge then slides forward under the rear section until the latter falls into place, locking automatically to form one continuous structure. The whole assembly is then pushed forward on a cantilever boom which is lowered when the bridge is clear of the chassis – depositing it at the far end first and then at the vehicle end. The Biber can then pull back and withdraw; alternatively after crossing the obstacle it can take up the bridge on the far side.

The bridge can span a gap of up to 20m (65ft) and can take vehicles up to 50tonne or, in an emergency, up to 60tonne. In sum, like the other members of the Leopard family, the Biber is efficient and tactically very effective. 105 are in service with the German Army, 14 have been supplied to the Netherlands, six to Canada and five each to Norway and Australia.

Above left and left: **Biber extending bridge.** *Both Krauss Maffei*

Above: **Biber bridgelayer in travelling order.** *Krauss Maffei*

Right: **Biber about to launch its bridge with the dozer blade being used as a brace.**

Left: **Prototype of the Matador twin 30mm anti-aircraft gun system on the Leopard 1 chassis; this was dropped in favour of the twin 35mm system.** *Rheinmetall*

Bottom: **Oerlikon 35mm KDA cannon as installed in Gepard.** *Oerlikon-Bührle*

Right and below right: **Views of the Gepard AA gun system.** *Krauss Maffei; BdV*

Armoured Anti-Aircraft Vehicle (Flakpanzer Gepard) *(For specification see p110)*

The most striking member of the Leopard 'family' is undoubtedly the anti-aircraft tank, the *Gepard* (Hunting Leopard). AA tanks are a relatively new post-World War 2 development, arising from German wartime experience with their panzer formations. Towards the end of the war in Europe Allied air superiority was such that it was almost impossible for the German columns to operate without protection against low-flying fighter-bombers. Development in the fields of electronics and aviation since 1945 have worsened the situation, as was seen in the 1973 Arab-Israeli war. So, towards the end of the 1950s the Bundeswehr decided that a new mobile AA weapon system should be developed capable of operating day and night in any kind of weather. This new AA tank, it was hoped, would replace between 1975 and 1977 the obsolete M42 AA tank then in service with the German Army. The military specification that was drawn up called for a weapon system with guns of between 20 and 44mm calibre which would be able to engage for at least two seconds a target suddenly appearing at a range of 3,000m.

Attempts to combine a 30mm twin gun with a fire control system on the chassis of an armoured personnel carrier (initially the HS30 APC and later on the Marder) were unsuccessful – primarily because the APC chassis was too small to take the complex fire control system needed. Some of the designers argued that it was not feasible to install both the AA guns with surveillance and fire control radars on the same vehicle, and suggested that it might be better to separate the functions completely and mount them on two armoured vehicles – one taking the radar and fire control and the other the AA guns; but

tactical considerations militated against this. Another consideration was that the larger chassis of the Leopard 1 seemed more promising than that of the APC. Thus it was that a number of firms teamed up to create the new AA tank on the Leopard chassis. In the event they produced two contending experimental prototypes. The first, offered by Rheinmetall GmbH and designated the Matador 30 ZFLA, was equipped with two 30mm Rheinmetall cannons, a Siemens surveillance radar and an AEG-Telefunken fire control radar. In June 1970 after extensive troop trials the Matador was rejected in favour of the second prototype which had been built as a collaborative venture by Oerlikon-Buhrle of Zurich, Contraves AG of Zurich and Siemens AG of Munich. This vehicle, equipped with two 35mm Oerlikon guns, with a range of 3,500m, was designated 5 PFZ-A; it was followed by the 5 PFZ-B which was redesignated the Gepard.

The Gepard's complete weapon system, comprising a search radar, a tracking radar, a computerised fire control system and the two 35mm guns, is housed either in or on the turret. Thus the vehicle is a completely self-contained unit capable of functioning independently. (It should be noted, however, that the tactical concept governing the employment of Gepard does not envisage a duel between one AA tank and a single aircraft. What is expected is that AA tanks will have to cope with a large number of aircraft attacking in rapid succession. In such circumstances

Views of the Gepard with radars deployed and (right) firing. Note spent 35mm cases in snow around vehicle. These are ejected from the top of the gun assembly – see photograph on p58.
Oerlikon-Bührle (3); Contraves

Four views of the Dutch version of Gepard, the CA1 Caesar, with tracking radars by Hollandse Signaalapparaten. (Right) Test-firing the 35mm cannon – note ejecting shell cases at right of photograph. (Above and far right) Two views of the CA1 showing the two sets of six smoke dischargers on either side of the turret (the German version has four). (Top right) Dutch CA1 prototype.
Hollandse Signaalapparaten BV(2); Krauss Maffei; Oerlikon-Bührle

Gepards will be more effective if they are linked by radio data channels into an area anti-aircraft defence system.)

In action the search radar carries out a continual surveillance, automatically interrogating all contacts with its built-in IFF facility. A hostile target is then displayed on the Gepard commander's screen and he designates it by means of an indicator which assigns a marker to the aircraft on the screen. A tracking radar at the front of the turret then takes over and a computer calculates the lead angle, taking into account the metereological conditions, the tilt-angle of the guns and speed of target, as well as calculating the optimum time and duration of the engagement in order to conserve the expenditure of ammunition. The target is then engaged by the two 35mm automatic Oerlikons which have a cyclic rate of fire of 550round/min.

The guns are mounted in armoured housings on the left and right side of the turret, and, as they are mounted externally, there are none of the usual problems of spent cartridge cases and noxious fumes. The guns are also

easily accessible for maintenance and repair. HE ammunition is used to engage hostile aircraft because of its fragmentation, blast and incendiary effects. However the guns can also be used in a ground role and kinetic energy rounds are carried for used against armoured targets.

The Gepard has a crew of three, commander, gunner and driver. The commander has overall responsibility in action while the gunner is primarily responsible for the operation of the fire control system (FCS) and guns. But the control console is so arranged as to make it possible for the commander and the gunner to exchange roles without actually changing position. To enable the commander to keep a check on the working of the FCS, fault indicator lamps are provided on the control; if an assembly or sub-system fails, or if the search radar is jammed by electronic countermeasures the commander decides which back-up facility is to be employed. The gunner's job is to engage the target indicated by the tank commander. And if the enemy tries to jam his fire control radar with electronic countermeasures he switches in the

appropriate electronic counter-countermeasure equipment. Finally the driver steers the tank according to orders issued by the commander, but it is largely up to him to position the tank with a good field of view and fire when the vehicle halts.

The Dutch Army bought 95 Gepards, and the Belgian Army has also purchased 55; their version of the vehicle, the CA1 is known as the Cheetah and is fitted with fire control equipment by Hollandse Signaalapparaten NV of Holland. The Germans have 420.

Other Projects

The foregoing derivatives of the Leopard are all in service, but the possibilities of using the Leopard chassis for other variants are by no means exhausted. Mention has been made of the suspended project for a 155mm SP gun using a turret developed in France. Other studies have considered the feasibility of armoured vehicles equipped with ground-to-ground and ground-to-air rockets. From a logistic as well as a training viewpoint such developments proffer considerable advantages. Other Leopard-based vehicles include the training tanks seen in a later chapter. Belgium and the Netherlands have taken 12 each, while the Germans have 60.

Below: **Early model of the Gepard with both tracking and surveillance radars retracted.** *Oerlikon-Bührle*

6. Leopard 2

While Leopard 1 was coming into service the Bundeswehr was considering not only the replacement of the 1,000 or so M48 tanks still in service with the German Army, but also the generation of tanks that would succeed Leopard 1. Clearly it would be to NATO's advantage if the design of the new tank could be standardised with Germany's allies.

So, in partnership with the United States, the Germans embarked on a joint programme to develop a new tank. This vehicle, known as the MBT-70/KPz70, actually reached the prototype stage. However the project ran into difficulties very early on and was abandoned in January 1970. Before this, however, the Germans had realised the way things were going and had in fact already started work on an independent project, designated initially Kampfpanzer 2, then *Keiler* (Wild Boar) and finally Leopard 2. In conjunction with Porsche, Wegmann and AEG-Telefunken, Krauss-Maffei built a couple of

Below and bottom: **The MBT-70, a joint German-American project, which reached prototype stage and taught the Germans valuable lessons put into practice in Leopard 2. For a specification of the MBT-70 see p111.** *General Motors; Krauss Maffei*

Top: **Kampfpanzer-70 – a line drawing of the German MBT-70 design.** *Krauss Maffei*

Above and below: **Prototype Leopard 2s with 120mm main gun and Leopard 1 style configuration.** *Krauss Maffei*

pre-prototypes and when the American/West German project was cancelled the Germans switched the funds to the Kampfpanzer 2 Keiler project, and experience gained in the ill-fated MBT-70 development work was embodied in the subsequent development.

The primary aim of the design team working on the Kampfpanzer 2 was to increase the firepower of the new MBT over that of Leopard 1, by mounting a better gun and developing an integrated fire control system; in developing the new fire control system all the components were designed so that they could eventually be fitted into the Leopard 1.

In 1972 the Bundeswehr authorised the production of 17 prototypes mounting a smoothbore gun. These were ready in 1973, and in the spring of 1974 they underwent extensive trials at Meppen, Munster and Trier. Four prototypes also underwent a series of cold weather trials at Camp Shilo in Canada, and then went on to the US Yuma Research Centre in Arizona for hot weather trials. All the vehicles completed the tests satisfactorily and were reported to have performed in an outstanding fashion.

These trials stimulated American interest again, and in December 1974 a Memorandum of Understanding (MoU) was concluded between the US and Germany in an attempt to 'harmonise' German and US tank development. The idea was to create a standard NATO MBT for the 1980s. Following more trials by the US Army at the Aberdeen Proving Ground the Americans declared that in their opinion the German fire control system was too complicated, that the armour protection was insufficient, and that the tank was too expensive. To be an acceptable contender to the American XM1, currently being developed by the Chrysler Company and General Motors, the Leopard 2 would have to incorporate certain alterations, simplifications and a few extras. (The American view was supposedly based on an analysis of the result of tank engagements in the Arab-Israeli October 1973 War, and recent developments in armour technology.) Accordingly the Leopard 2 was redesigned and a new version, the Leopard 2AV (*Austere Version,* sometimes known as the *Amerikanische Version*) appeared in 1976. The designation 'Austere' is in fact misleading as the word implies the elimination of frills and unnecessary extras, and the performance of this version of the Leopard 2 has not been affected.

The most significant difference between the 'Austere' prototypes and the other German Leopard 2 prototypes was in the turret which in the case of the Leopard 2AV presents a box-like appearance.

Two versions of the 'Austere' prototypes were displayed, one mounting the Rheinmetall 120mm smoothbore gun, the second armed with the 105mm L7A3 gun for comparative trials with the XM1. It was because of these trials in September to December 1976 that the Austere prototypes were produced in a hurry. The evaluation of the results was never disclosed but it may well be that the Americans had already decided that they preferred their own Chrysler-made XM1. Both the US and Germany agreed that 'harmonisation' was still desirable however, and that – so far as possible – items such as the main armament, ammunition, the powerpack, fire control system and so on ought to be standardised.*

* Those who have had any experience of attempts to standardise other equipment in NATO will be sceptical about this pious wish.

Below and following pages: **The Leopard 2AV armed with 105mm and 120mm (p66 bottom left) main guns. While the 2AV never got further than the prototype stage, it was the direct link between the Leopard 1 and 2 production types and superseded the other Leopard 2 prototype configuration shown in photos on p62. Note different MG mountings on the vehicles.** *Krauss Maffei; BdV (1)*

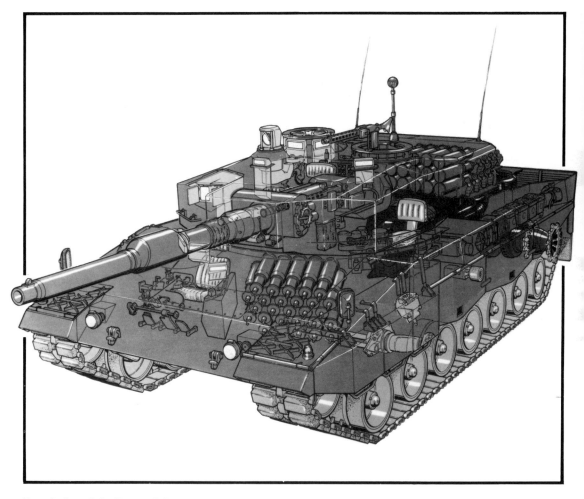

Description of the Leopard 2

(For specifications see p111)

Like its forerunner, Leopard 1, the Leopard 2 is conventional in layout and design; all its components and the techniques used in its production are based on well-tried technology. The overall result is a reliable and efficient armoured fighting vehicle with an outstanding performance which, if the occasion ever arises, should acquit itself well in battle.

Both the hull and turret of the Leopard 2 are of all-welded construction and the front of the hull and the turret are said to 'combine steels of various hardness and elastic materials' in novel multi-layer armour (a combination of spaced and Chobham armours). For protection against mines the hull floor has been reinforced and external edges sloped at an angle of 45°. Ammunition stowed in the turret is in an ejectable basket in the turret bulge; the hydraulic gun and turret control system is also contained in the turret bulge.

The main armament is the Rheinmetall 120mm, smoothbore gun, which has a drop block breach and a hydraulically assisted loading mechanism. The 120mm smoothbore is the first such gun to be mounted on a NATO tank. A hydraulic loading system is necessary because the rounds – which are in one piece combining cartridge and projectile – are very heavy. It fires two types of ammunition – Armour-Piercing Fin-Stabilised Discarding Sabot (APFSDS) and a general purpose HE round (known as MZ); in essence the latter is a shaped charge HEAT round that can be used against both lightly armoured targets or to support infantry. The cartridges are partly combustible. The bore of the gun is chromium plated and the life of the barrel sleeve is said to be about 1,000 rounds although, during tests, accuracy started to fall off after about 400 rounds had been fired. Secondary armament consists of a 7.62mm coaxial machine gun, another 7.62mm machine gun for AA use, eight grenade launchers and eight smoke pots.

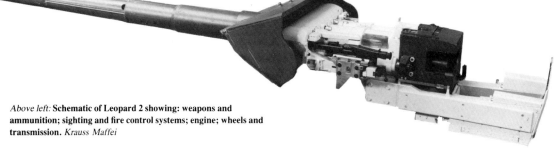

Above left: **Schematic of Leopard 2 showing: weapons and ammunition; sighting and fire control systems; engine; wheels and transmission.** *Krauss Maffei*

Top: **Roll-out of the first production Leopard 2 for the German Army, October 1979.** *Christopher F. Foss*

Right: **Detail of Leopard 2's Rheinmetall 120mm smoothbore main gun and coaxial machine gun assembly.** *Rheinmetall*

The gun-laying and stabilisation systems are improved versions of those developed for the Leopard 1, ie the Cadillac Gage electro-hydraulic turret traverse system. The electronically controlled fire control system has been

refined, and while the first 17 prototypes carried Zeiss EMES-12 combined laser-stereoscopic rangefinders, the Leopard 2AV vehicles were fitted with a Hughes stabilised rangefinder. (This change led to the redesign of the turret and the provision of multiple space armour.) This is manufactured under licence by Krupp Atlas-Elektronic. The gunner also has a x8 monocular auxiliary telescope; the commander a panoramic periscope for sighting. Eight periscopes are available to the commander while the driver has three.

For night operations the Leopard 2 is fitted with passive night vision devices and a white light/infra-red searchlight. The Leopard 2 is powered by a 12-cylinder MTU Ka501 multi-fuel engine which develops an output of 1,500hp. For the size of the engine this is a very high output and although the tank weighs more than 50,000kg it has an extremely favourable power/weight ratio of 27.3hp/ton. Two exhaust gas turbochargers – one for each bank of cylinders – are the main contributory factor to the high power output. The cooling system is assisted by two large circular coolers with concentric radial fans located over the gearbox; this permits full load operation at temperatures up to +30°C. The fuel capacity is 1,320litre (348gal) which gives the vehicle a cruising range of 400km on roads and 250km over medium-heavy terrain. With pre-heating the engine can be started at temperatures down to –30°C, and a complete engine change can be effected in about 12-15min.

The transmission is a Renk HSWL-354/5 type incorporating the steering unit. This is described as 'combined stepless hydrostatic regenerative', having a four-speed planetary gearbox fitted with a bypass clutch.

The suspension is the classic torsion bar type, with seven road wheels and four support idlers on each side. The principal idler is in front and the drive sprocket at the rear. There are five shock absorbers on each side – fitted to all the road wheel stations except the fourth and fifth. New low-vibration tracks fitted with detachable rubber track pads have been developed for Leopard 2 and it is claimed that these improve the performance of the stabilised optical systems.

For NBC protection the Leopard 2 is fitted with a pressurised system supplemented by air filters which can be changed from the outside.

As mentioned earlier the Americans backed away from a decision to adopt Leopard 2 in favour of their own XM1; this effectively ended the attempt to create a standard NATO MBT as a whole. Development continued on national lines, and the objective now was to standardise components and make them interchangeable. A US decision to adopt a 120mm calibre gun appeared to be a sensible contribution to this ideal although it did not

Left: **Early Leopard 2 prototype armed with 120mm main gun and Rh202 20mm cannon at commander's station.** *Krauss Maffei*

necessarily ensure that the Americans would use the German gun in the XM1. They were supposed to have decided this in January 1977, after comparative trials of the Rheinmetall weapon and the British 120mm gun mounted in the Chieftain. When the time came however the Americans postponed their decision until the end of December 1977, and as soon as the news reached Bonn the German Ministry of Defence approved the installation of the Rheinmetall smoothbore in the Leopard 2. A few months later, in mid-1977, the Defence Minister, Herr Georg Leber, asked for and obtained parliamentary approval to procure 1,800 Leopard 2s to replace the 1,054 M48A2 tanks currently in the Bundeswehr inventory. The price tag was said to be roughly DM6.5billion (£1,625million) suggesting that the cost of a single Leopard 2 is approximately £1million. This is a very high cost indeed and is probably an overestimate. (In this connection it is interesting to note that in 1976 a consortium of American firms interested in producing the Leopard 2 in the USA under licence undertook a study of

Right: **One of the first three MaK advanced series Leopard 2s delivered to the Bundeswehr. Note the three small lifting side plates which distinguish the Leopard 2 from the prototypes and 2AV version.** *Krauss Maffei*

Below: **Pre-production Leopard 2 hull on Elefant transporter sent to the German Army for training.** *Krauss Maffei*

the cost. After calculating the manufacture of all components under production conditions the study group concluded that a Leopard 2 would cost $811,226 (1976 prices). $27,900 of this sum was for licensing fees.) Technical performance apart, the cost of new equipment inevitably plays an important role, and some of the other NATO countries which have expressed interest in Leopard 2 as a successor to Leopard 1 may well be deterred by the price. The first three pre-production Leopard 2s were delivered to the German Army late in 1978 without turrets for training purposes. In October 1979 they took possession of the first of their projected 1,800 Leopard 2s, and anticipate that the order will be filled by 1986. MaK, Kiel will build 810 and Krauss-Maffei 990. In March 1979 the Dutch placed an order for 445, to be delivered 1982-86, to replace their ageing Centurions and AMX-13s. Other countries, including Belgium and Switzerland have already expressed an interest in Leopard 2.

Leopard 2 Derivatives
Plans and feasibility studies exist only for Leopard 2 variants – and the only concrete plan is for an AEV. It is likely that an ARV will be built and possible that the Gepard turret could be mounted on the Leopard 2 chassis.

73

Above: **Rear view showing differences between the Leopard 2 (left) and Leopard 1A3.**
Krauss Maffei

Right: **Leopard 2 with turret to rear and front skirt plates raised.**
Krauss Maffei

7. Servicing and Maintenance

In battle the time and effort needed to service and maintain combat equipment is of decisive significance. When a vehicle breaks down or is damaged it must be made operational again as quickly as possible. This means repairing or replacing defective components and the easier this is to do, the sooner the vehicle will be back in service. In view of the complexity of modern equipment it is generally quicker to replace defective components or groups of components and leave their repair to skilled personnel in workshops outside the combat area. In consequence when the Leopard and its derivatives were designed a number of components were grouped together to constitute units which could be easily replaced on the battlefield. For example in the event of an engine or a transmission failure in the Leopard three men in a matter of only about 20min can replace the complete

Two views of the Leopard ARV during maintenance operations; (below) Lifting an early production Leopard 1 and (overleaf) with Leopard 1 powerpack. Note deployment of ARV dozer blade. *BdV: Krauss Maffei*

powerpack with a spare powerpack carried on the engine compartment deck plate of the armoured recovery vehicle. Similarly it takes only about 15min to fit new brake linings and a turret can be replaced in 2hr.

Most of the normal servicing and maintenance of the Leopard can be carried out by the crew with tools carried on the tank. A few spare parts also are carried on the individual tank and these enable the crew to cope with minor defects. Retensioning the tracks, for instance, or replacing the individual track links, road wheels or sprockets takes them only a few minutes.

Major servicing, maintenance and repair tasks are

carried out by the army workshops and special tools have been developed to facilitate the maintenance programme which has been worked out for the Leopard. In the event every effort has been made to reduce the time spent on maintenance and Krauss-Maffei claim that no major overhaul is needed under 10,000km of operation. On this basis and the assumption that a Leopard has a lifespan of 20 years and covers an average of 1,000km per year, only two major overhauls will be needed in the vehicle's entire lifespan. (This assessment has been based on the wear rate estimated by the German Army following experience with the early Leopards.)

8. Training Aids

A considerable amount of instructional equipment has been developed to facilitate the training of Leopard crews and maintenance personnel. Apart from the customary run of films, photographs and charts, full scale wooden mock-ups with dummy components identical with those on a real Leopard have been devised. For example to introduce and familiarise those designated as drivers of the Leopard with their role, wooden mock-ups of the forward part hull section have been constructed. These are open in the middle so that a small class of learner drivers can watch while one of their number takes his turn on this stationary 'driver's station'. Using a special control panel the instructor can simulate various conditions which the student can identify on the

instrument panel in front of him. This enables him to grasp the rudiments of his task, and effects a great saving in terms of time and money compared with instructions on a real tank.

Having graduated from the stationary mock-up, the embryo driver continues his instruction on a 'driving school tank'. In effect this is a modified Leopard, with a special cab mounted on the chassis in place of the turret. A balance ring compensates for turret weight and in all other respects this driving school vehicle has exactly the same characteristics as the real tank. Indeed it is even capable of crossing water obstacles, so that student drivers get used to fording operations. The cab is roomy enough for one driver under instruction, the instructor,

Above right: **Leopard driving school vehicle as used by Belgian and Dutch armies.** *Krauss Maffei*

Right: **Leopard driver training vehicle with dummy gun barrel attachment as used by German Army.** *Krupp MaK*

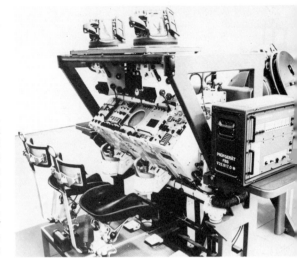

and two other trainees who are there merely to observe. The cab has glass windows which permit the instructor a clear all-round view. Two instrument panels are provided – one for the learner-driver, the second for the instructor; this enables the latter to monitor the trainee's performance. If the trainee does something wrong the instructor can override him from his own seat in the cab and take over complete control of the vehicle – steering, braking, gear-shifting and accelerating. The instructor and the learner driver are able to communicate by means of the intercom system and the two observer trainees can listen in to their conversation.

During his training on the driving school tank the trainee learns what to expect when he moves on to a Leopard proper. However a further training aid, a driving simulator, is also available to supplement his 'on-vehicle' training and simulators have proved to be extremely successful in expanding the scope of a driver's training. They have also cut the cost of training a driver since less vehicles are needed and consequently the wear and tear on combat equipment is reduced. But, apart from the economic benefit deriving from the use of simulators, there are other advantages, since training is not dependent on weather or other external factors such as the availability of training grounds.

A simulator to train a tank driver consists of a scale model (the scale is normally 1:300) of 'driving terrain' and a driver's cab, the interior equipment of which is an exact replica of that which confronts the driver in the Leopard. From the driver's cab the trainee driver steers a scale model tank across the surface of the 'terrain', on which roads, trees and houses provide a realistic picture of the countryside on which the Leopard is supposed to be operating. The model is free to move according to the

driver's directions or along predetermined paths determined by information supplied by a linked computer. Various road and terrain conditions, operating noises etc are stored in the computer and transmitted to the driver in accordance with a particular 'driving' situation. Sitting in his cab, with the hatch open or closed, the driver operates his vehicle using a television camera. His reactions are fed into the computer which compares them with the terrain, steers the model tank across the terrain and refers the pitch and roll that would be experienced by the model back to the cab. Simulated driving noises are also fed back to the cab and together with its movement give the trainee a realistic impression of what he would experience of the environmental conditions associated with his particular exercise.

The instructor is provided with a television monitor on which he can observe the terrain in front of the vehicle, and he can vary the operating conditions to simulate wet or icy roads and changes in the rolling condition. He can also introduce simulated mechanical problems such as steering and braking malfunctions and a shortage of fuel.

All events occurring during the simulated driving exercises are recorded, to facilitate the discussion of mistakes made by the trainee driver and to compare the performance of individual drivers.

For gunnery training other aids have been developed. To familiarise Leopard crews and maintenance personnel with the 105mm gun a 'gun mounting' is available. This consists simply of a gun and its associated equipment on a mobile platform. The gun cannot actually be fired but it can be elevated and traversed in exactly the same way as

in the tank; recoil and return movements of the gun tube are simulated by means of a hydraulic retraction mechanism.

After the loader has mastered the lessons of loading the gun at different elevations on the 'gun mounting', he moves on to what can best be described as a training turret. This is a mobile structure consisting of a complete Leopard turret on a tubular steel rig. Connected to the mains power supply through a transformer, the turret can be used for gun laying. The main gun itself cannot be fired but it is possible to conduct practice shoots with the coaxial and AA machine guns. Furthermore a 20mm gun can be mounted coaxially on the main tube, and this allows practice firings at ranges of up to 1,300m. (As the ballistic characteristics of the 20mm rounds are very similar to the 105mm HESH ammunition at medium ranges the optical sight can be used without any modification.) Normally however gunnery training on the main armament is done with small calibre weapons; this enables shoots to be conducted on miniature ranges. The coaxial machine gun is dismounted and replaced by either a 14.5mm gun, which can fire tracer ammunition with an impact fuse up to 150mm or the smaller calibre KK22 unit which allows a target range of between 20 and 50m. With 14.5mm unit the sighting devices on the main gun have to be modified to compensate for ballistic deviations; this is done with prisms. For the KK22 unit, however, no parallax correction is needed.

For more advanced gunnery training an electronic firing simulator – similar to the driving simulator – has been developed. Known as the TALISSI (Tactical Light

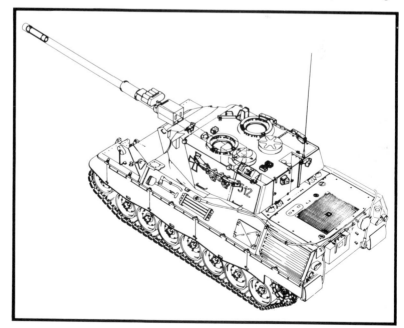

Left: **Wegmann gun turret trainer. Equipped with turret hydraulics, electrical system and optical components, it basically trains personnel in electronic maintenance. A movement simulator simulates hull movement.** *Wegmann*

Right: **Talissi – tactical light shot simulator – showing main components. With a 'flash, bang, smoke' pyrotechnic charge indicating firing, the main system is based on a laser emitter and optical receiver.** *Kurt Eichweber AG*

Shot Simulator) and produced by Kurt Eighweben, of Hamburg, a firm which specialises in laser communications, 720 have been ordered for the German Army. Of it, the Commander in Chief, Lt-Gen Horst Hildebrandt, has written, 'it forces the crew to behave as in combat. Thus, the troops are able to a great extent, realistically to reproduce tank combat during manoeuvres, in every type of terrain and outside the training grounds.' Basically the TALISSI consists of a cab mounted on a movable platform, which can simulate the motions of a Leopard on the move. The cab is fitted out like the turret of a Leopard and – as with the driving simulator – a model serves to depict a typical stretch of operational terrain. On the model there are fixed and moving targets which can be fired at from the cab. Four commanders and gunners can be trained on the simulator at the same time.

The actual 'firing' of a round is simulated in a computer into which is fed the gun laying data and information concerning the gun, ammunition and environmental conditions. The computer calculates the penetration point on the model and hits are identified by a light spot on the model; to evaluate the accuracy of the round the spot can be 'frozen'.

The model is so designed as to make it feasible for practice shoots at simulated ranges of between 500 and 300m. And the fact that this can be done in barracks under classroom conditions obviously has considerable advantages. Apart from the training not being restricted by weather and the availability of an adequate range, 105mm (and 120mm) ammunition is very expensive so there is a considerable saving in cost. Indeed as the simulation of movement, illumination and noise is so realistic it is possible to train a Leopard crew to 'feel' exactly what it is like to fire the main armament without actually having to participate in a live firing shoot in a tank.

Finally there is the question of the training of those who maintain the vehicles. For this a variety of equipment has been developed to simulate almost every conceivable malfunction – mechanical failures, and faults in the electrical system, electronics, optics and hydraulics. The fault-finding equipment has been designed for use by men who do not have any specialised scientific knowledge, and its prime purpose is to facilitate the detection and identification of the malfunction which can then be dealt with in accordance with a 'drill' laid down in a technical manual.

Below: **A Leopard 1 fitted with Simfire showing laser projector fitted to the gun barrel, the flash generator which controls the 'bang, flash, smoke' effects, the radio transmitter/receiver which responds to the Simfire attack signal and two of the four detectors which pick up the laser signal (on turret sides). For a full description of Simfire and Simfics see** *Modern Combat Vehicles 1 – Chieftain. Solartron*

9. The Leopard compared with other MBTs

In comparing the Leopard with other battle tanks the development criteria which were discussed earlier need to be borne in mind. Soviet tank designers, for example, place equal emphasis on firepower, armour protection and cross-country mobility, the British and the Americans put firepower, armour protection and mobility in that order of priority, while tank designers in Europe (except the UK, but including West Germany) regard mobility as being more important than armour. In brief the outcome of these different concepts has been that the Warsaw Pact armies, equipped mainly by the Soviet Union, have a huge inventory of a very few types of tank which are simply designed, rugged, relatively cheap and – by Western standards – uncomfortable for the crews that man them. The West's tanks on the other hand are, by and large, of better quality and have a better performance; they are more sophisticated and more complex. But the differing concepts that have influenced their design have militated against standardisation and created for NATO a host of logistic problems.

The technical data relating to the tanks in this comparison are listed in the table at the end of this chapter. The most important ones are the US M60, the British Chieftain, the French AMX-30, the Swedish Strv103B, the Swiss Pz61/58 and the Soviet T62 and T72.

On the basis of armament alone the T72, with its 125mm smoothbore gun firing fin-stabilised ammunition

M60A1 – the current American MBT – evolved from a 1944 design, the M26 Pershing, via the M46, M47 and M48. While it has all the conventional modern 'add-on' aids – laser rangefinder, stabilisation, electronic fire control system – it is nevertheless an improvement of an old design, sound rather than spectacular. It is armed with the British 105mm main gun. The photograph shows an M60A1 in Germany. *US Army*

is probably superior to all the West's tanks including the Leopard 1. But the performance of the Leopard 2's gun may well match the Soviet weapon, as may that of the Chieftain's 120mm. However, the T72 is only just coming into service and the majority of tanks of the Warsaw Pact armies are T54/55s or T62s. While the older T54/55s still have a 100mm gun the T62 mounts a 115mm smoothbore weapon. Whether this 115mm gun can match the British 105mm high-performance gun* – with which the Leopard, the M60A1 and the Centurion are equipped – is questionable. Like the Soviet 100mm the British 105mm can fire three standard types of ammunition – APDS, HEAT and HESH. The French AMX-30 is also equipped with a 105mm gun, but this is a weapon developed in France, designed primarily to fire fin-stabilised HEAT rounds. The greater firepower of the British Chieftain may be marginally superior to that of Leopard 1 but it will equate to that of the Leopard 2. The Chieftain was in fact designed and developed as an MBT with a gun accurate over long ranges but with sufficient armour protection for short range engagements. These requirements resulted in increased vehicle weight, greater vehicle width, reduced mobility and a smaller supply of ammunition.

* The Swiss 61/68 tank, the Swedish Strv103B, the Vickers MK3, and the Japanese St-B tank are also equipped with a modified version of the British gun.

With the exception of the US M60A1, the French AMX-30, the Swedish Strv103B and the Swiss Pz61 all the battle tanks in this comparison have a weapon stabilisation system. (A stabilisation system has been tested for the AMX-30 but has not yet been introduced. The Americans are retro fitting the M60A1 with the system used in the M60A2.) The Swedish tank has no turret and its gun is rigidly installed; elevation and traverse are accomplished by means of hydropneumatic suspension or infinitely variable cross-drive. The vehicle has a very low silhouette and automatic loading allows a high rate of fire. The turretless tank is a novel concept whilst the Leopard, which is based firmly on existing technology, is by no means a revolutionary fighting vehicle. But the Swedish tank has encountered many teething problems while the Leopard has had a relatively clear passage from the design stage.

Below: **Chieftain. While there are doubts about its automotive reliability, which certainly reduces its effectiveness, the Chieftain's weaponry and fire control system is amongst the best in the world.** *Martin Horseman*

The current Swiss MBT is the Pz68 (below right), an improved version of the earlier Pz61 (right). Armed with the British 105mm main gun, lighter than most other European MBTs, the Pz68 has been designed for use in Switzerland's mountainous terrain. Note the Pz61's 20mm cannon coaxial with main armament and the Pz68's 7.5mm machine gun mounted coaxially. *Both Swiss Army*

Left: **T54Bs of the Soviet Army on manoeuvres. Developed from the earlier T44, the T54 is armed with a 100mm main gun. Outdated now, it has been superseded by both the T62 and T72 (above). The latter has a different chassis – a departure from the T34/44/54/62 series – and is armed with a 125mm main gun which is fed from an automatic loader thus allowing a reduction of the crew to three.** *Tass; US Army*

In the Leopard the gunner has an extremely powerful optical rangefinder with a 1,720mm base and ×16 magnification, which permits satisfactory ranging, aiming and firing – even in poor visibility. Most of the comparable tanks have optical rangefinders controlled by the tank commander whereas that with which the Leopard is equipped is also the gunner's primary sight, and the fact that the gunner can do the ranging and sighting gives the commander more latitude to concentrate on the tactical aspects of an engagement. A spotting machine gun is used on the British Chieftain; this is a simpler and cheaper method of ranging and the system was tested in the early stages of the development of the Leopard. The technique was rejected by the German experts, however, on the grounds that it was too slow and not sufficiently accurate at long combat ranges.

In nearly all tanks under review the gunners have ×8 monocular telescopes. But the Leopard has a rotatable panoramic ×6-×20 power telescope through which the tank commander can aim and range targets as well as observe the terrain even in poor light. In this respect the Leopard is unique. In its night capability also the German tank is superior. Except for the Swiss and Japanese vehicles all the tanks are equipped with infra-red devices to enable them to aim, shoot and drive at night. In the Leopard however the commander's panoramic telescope can be replaced by an infra-red sight which operates in conjunction with an infra-red searchlight.

In terms of mobility the Leopard is superior to all other tanks, of which all but one are equipped with liquid-cooled diesel or multi-fuel engines. (The exception is the American M60 which has an air-cooled diesel.) The Leopard 2 with a top speed of 72km/h can outrun the rest and, although the Russians claim a maximum speed of 100km/h for the T72, even with a new engine and improved suspension to that of the T62, 60km/h would be more believable. Even the Leopard 1 with a top speed of 65km/h – the same as that of the AMX-30 – has a 10km/h or more advantage over the T62 and the M60 and 5km/h over the new Chieftain. The radius of action is another mobility factor, and here again the Leopard scores. The cruising range of the Leopard – and the AMX-30 – is 600km, while that of the T72 is 500 and of the old T62 a mere 350km, although this can be increased to 630km by fitting expendable auxiliary fuel tanks.

Besides a very creditable engine performance the mobility of the Leopard can be attributed to the transmission of the power the engine develops. The electro-hydraulic steer/shift transmission permits effort-less clutch-free shifting without interrupting the flow of power. From the driver's viewpoint also this is important as a driver controlling a tank with automatic transmission suffers none of the fatigue to which tank drivers operating transmissions with clutch pedals were subjected in the past. The driver with the automatic transmission will thus be able to concentrate more of his attention on the battle.

A high power-to-weight ratio is another consideration in the Leopard's favour. That of the Leopard 2 is 27.7hp/ton; only the American XM1 which is expected to be taken into service in late 1980/early 1981 has a higher ratio – 28.8hp/ton. (The Chieftain Mk 5 has a particularly low power/weight ratio, 13.6hp/ton; owing to the priority given to armour protection when it was designed. Taking into account the fact that its maximum speed is only 44km/h it has been suggested that the British tank is 'sluggish'. That may be an exaggeration but it is certainly distinctly less mobile than the Leopard and AMX-30.) The 27.7hp/ton power-to-weight ratio gives the Leopard considerable acceleration and in conjunction with the vehicle's suspension system this results in outstanding cross-country mobility.)

In terms of mobility the Leopard is superior to all other tanks, of which all but one are equipped with liquid-cooled diesel or multi-fuel engines. (The exception is the American M60 which has an air-cooled diesel). The Leopard 2 with a top speed of 72km/h can outrun the rest and, although the Russians claim a maximum speed of 100km/h for the T72, even with a new engine and improved suspension to that of the T62 60km/h would be more believable. Even the Leopard 1 with a top speed of 65km/h – the same as that of the AMX-30 – has a 10km/h or more advantage over the T62 and the M60 and 5km/h over the new Chieftain. The radius of action is another mobility factor, and here again the Leopard scores. The cruising range of the Leopard – and the AMX-30 – is 600km, while that of the T72 is 500 and of the old T62 a mere 350km, although this can be increased to 630km by fitting expendable auxiliary fuel tanks.

Besides a very creditable engine performance the mobility of the Leopard can be attributed to the transmission of the power the engine develops. The electro-hydraulic steer/shift transmission permits effort-less clutch-free shifting without interrupting the flow of power. From the driver's viewpoint also this is important as a driver controlling a tank with automatic transmission suffers none of the fatigue to which tank drivers operating manual transmissions with clutch pedals were subjected in the past. The driver with the automatic transmission will thus be able to concentrate more of his attention on the battle.

The weight and width of a tank are important when considering traffic limitations – the strength of bridges and the problems of road and rail transport. As far as vehicle weight is concerned Leopard 1 was nearer the ideal than Leopard 2 (at 54.1ton) which is about the same weight of the Mk 5 Chieftain and only marginally less heavy than the new Chieftain. As a comparison the combat weight of the T72 is only 40ton – a figure which has been specified as the development goal for tanks of the West. With a width of 3.25m the Leopard is narrower than the M60 (3.63m), the Chieftain (3.50m including

armour skirts) and the T72 (3.39m), but broader than the AMX-30, which is only 3.10m wide. (Narrowest of all the modern battle tanks is the Swiss Pz61 (3.05m) which was built for service in mountainous regions where there is a predominance of narrow winding roads. Its successor, the Pz68, was made broader (3.15m) because the fighting compartment of the Pz61 proved to be too narrow and cramped.)

As might be expected the tank with the lowest silhouette is the turretless Swedish vehicle, the Strv103B, with an overall height of only 2.10m. The T62 (2.40m) is next; its successor the T72 is 2.80m tall while the Chieftain and AMX-30 both have an overall height of 2.86m. With a height of 2.62m the Leopard takes an in between position.

Comparing the armour protection of different tanks is

Right: **The American Army's next MBT is the XM1 Abrams still under development. Their first MBT not based on the M26 evolutionary chain, the XM1 is armed with a 105mm main gun, has Chobham armour and should prove equal to any MBT of the next generation.** *Chrysler*

difficult for two reasons. First because the actual thickness and composition of the armour plate is often classified information, but secondly and more importantly because the effectiveness of modern high explosive anti-tank projectiles is such that they will defeat practically any thickness of armour. Furthermore the latest anti-tank guided missiles increase the probability of a hit. It is of course possible to increase ballistic protection by making the armour thicker but this entails increased vehicle weight with a consequent reduction in mobility. And the German designers are among those who believe that speed of movement provides good protection for a tank. Thus with Leopard they have concentrated on armour shape, the avoidance of ballistic traps, and sandwich and spaced armour.

Compared with other tanks conditions inside the Leopard's crew compartment are good. The controls are easily accessible and easy to operate, while the automatic transmission and suspension systems alleviate the problem of driver fatigue. In the Soviet tanks, in particular, human engineering considerations have been given less attention, and it is true to say that the T54/55 fires and moves under conditions that Western tank crews would regard as intolerable.

If there are any criticisms of the German MBT they will inevitably be focused on the complexity and cost of the vehicle. One notable feature of modern Soviet tank designs is their relative simplicity compared with the tanks of the West. The T72, for example, has unpadded tracks and an uncomplicated transmission system; such features may have some tactical disadvantages but logistically they are beneficial.

Left: **Shir 2 with Chobham armour and 120mm main gun. The Shir will not see service with the British Army although it is the direct link between Chieftain and Challenger, the British next generation MBT.**

Below: **The current French MBT, the AMX-30, was produced after French/German attempts to build a common vehicle fell through. Armed with a 105mm main gun, the AMX-30 has a top speed of 65km/h and a range of 600km – in many ways it compares favourably to Leopard 1.** *Christopher F. Foss*

Turning now to costs: The following list shows in round figures the approximate cost of some of the tanks:*

	£	US$
T62	165,000	365,000
M60A1	205,000	450,000
Chieftain	255,000	560,000
M60A2	285,000	625,000
AMX-30	320,000	700,000
Leopard 1A4	395,000	870,000
Leopard 2	575,000	1,265,000
XM1	575,000	

* These figures were compiled from an estimate undertaken by the German Society for Military Technology and published by Wehr und Wissen, Koblenz/Bonn in the journal *Military Technology and Economics*, Issue 1.

The obvious deduction is that the less sophisticated Eastern bloc tanks cost far less than those of the West. What may not be appreciated is that a Soviet tank costs far less than its Western counterpart because of the low production quantities in the West. Which brings us to the final point in this comparison: some 6,000 or so Leopards will be in service with seven NATO armies over the next decade, and these tanks have been referred to as a 'corner-stone' of land defence in Western Europe. The Leopard is unquestionably an excellent and versatile fighting vehicle. But the Warsaw Pact armies can field close on 60,000 tanks while those of NATO and France togethar have a total inventory of 23,000; 10,000 of these are American, many of which are located in the United States. To equalise the odds therefore the Leopard needs to be at least three times as good as the T72. As the Leopard has not so far fired a single shot in anger, it is not possible to make such an assertion.

10. In foreign service

Above: **Australian Leopard 1A3 with dozer blade.** *Paul Handel*

Left: **Leopard 1 of the Belgian Army being unloaded from an American-made, Belgian-manned, mobile assault bridge.**

Above left: **Leopard 1 of the Belgian Army. Note the commander's FN machine gun in place of the German MG3. The Belgians took 334 Leopard MBTs, a number of which were fitted with the SABCA fire control system.** *Belgian Army*

Left: **Leopard ARV of the Dutch Army showing clearly nose and hull side details – note the brackets for various tools and the access hatch. If compared with a similar view of the AEV one can see the difference between the two vehicles in that an attachment has been bolted over the access cover. This is part of the heat exchanger which enables the AEV to use its hydraulic system at high ambient temperatures for extended periods of time. The Dutch took 52 ARVs.** *Dutch Army*

Above: **Leopard 1s of the Norwegian Army.** *Norwegian Army*

Below: **Leopard 1 of the Dutch Army, who took 468 MBTs. Note the lack of a thermal sleeve on the 105mm main gun, different exhaust louvres at rear, stowage boxes (a Dutch modification) on hull side and Dutch smoke dischargers on the turret. The Dutch use their own dischargers on their version of Leopard – a framework with six dischargers in three sets of two whereas the Germans have four single pots.** *Dutch Army*

In 1978 there was a major exercise in Norway, 'Arctic Express '78' which brought together Norwegian forces assigned to NATO's Allied Forces North Europe (AFNORTH) and elements of the ACE Mobile Force – multi-national conventional land and air forces capable of short-notice deployment to any part of the NATO area at times of crisis. The Norwegian forces included Leopard 1s of the medium tank squadron (Stridsvogneskadron) assigned to the Troms Land Defence District. This series of photographs from the exercise by Martin Horseman shows: (above left) a Bergepanzer (Leopard ARV) with camouflage netting and crewman completing his toilet! He is sitting on the jib-boom while two others of the crew of four are in their hatches. Note MG3 at commander's hatch and dozer blade in folded position at front. The squadron's tanks are named after racehorses and (centre left) a detail of the name *Batzeba* is seen on the turret side. Below: Leopards heading towards Vollan. Right and below right: Leopards deploying alongside a road awaiting the next move in the exercise. Note the Hoffman-Werke AG gunfire simulator on the 105mm gun barrel. This simulates visibly and audibly AFVs' gunfire by igniting electrically (by the operation of the 105mm's release mechanism) a pyrotechnic charge.

Two more views from the exercise:
Leopard under camouflage (above).
The netting is removed from the
AFV in a fixed position to allow easy
turret traverse; (right) another
Leopard called *Ulan*.

11. In German service

Left: **Gepard – 420 are in German Army service. Note surveillance radar erected – when retracted it swings back and down to lie horizontally over the engine decks.** *BdV*

Below: **Leopard 1A2 – note the thermal sleeve on 105mm main gun and side skirts.** *RAC Centre*

Above: **Leopard 1A1A1 on exercise showing clearly the spaced armour on turret and mantlet, early exhaust louvres and rubber side skirts.**

Left and below left: **Two views of a heavily camouflaged Leopard 1A4.**

Right: **Views of German Army Leopard 1A4s at speed. Right hand vehicle (centre) has searchlight in position.**

Left: **Leopard 1A4 with searchlight attached. Note commander's panoramic telescope, part of the integrated fire control system on this version of Leopard.**

Below: **Leopard 1A2 in muddy terrain.** *MTU*

Right: **Leopard 1A4s.** *MTU*

Below right: **Side view of German Army Leopard 1A4.** *Krauss Maffei*

Above: **Leopard 1 (third production batch) at gunnery practice.**
Krauss Maffei

Left: **Early production Leopard 1.**
BdV

Right: **Pioneerpanzer (AEV) using its bulldozer. Note driver's position and hull side detail differences from the Bergepanzer (ARV) – the ladder on the jib-boom (although this is occasionally removed), auger just visible behind the boom on the rear decks and the modified cover on the middle of the hull.** *Krupp MaK*

Right: **Biber bridgelayer in travelling order.** *Krauss Maffei*

Below: **End of Exercise 'Fore Front' in 1971. Nearest to the camera are early production Leopard 1s (note verticals on exhaust louvres) with later versions in middle distance. Also on parade are SPZ 12-3 APCs, Leopard ARVs, M113s, M109s, M48 AVLBs, while in the far distance are Chieftains.**

Appendices
1. Comparison of MBTs

A Western Powers

Country:	USA	USA	USA	UK	UK	UK	FRG	FRG	France	Sweden	Switzer-land	Japan
Type:	M60A1	M60A2	XM1	Vickers Mk 3	Chieftain Mk 5	Chieftain new	Leopard 1A4	Leopard 2	AMX-30	Strv 103B	Pz61/68	STB74
Combat weight: (tons)	48	51.9	52.1	38.7	54	55.5	42,4	54,1	36	39	38/39	38
Power-to weight ratio: (kW/ton (hp/ton))	11.4 (15.5)	10.6 (14.4)	22.2 (28.8)	14.0 (19)	10.0 (13.6)	15.9 (21.6)	14.5 (19.7)	20.4 (27.7)	14.7 (19.5)	13.8 (18.7)	12.5 (17)	14.5 (19.7)
Maximum speed: (km/h)	48	48	70	50	44	60	65	72	65	50	50/55	53
Radius: (km)	500	450	360	480	450	450	600	450	600	390	300/350	
Main gun calibre: (mm)	105	152	105	105	120	120	105	120	105	105	105	105
No of rounds:	63	13 guided missiles 33 con-ventional rounds	40	65	53	53	55 (AS1 and C1 59)	40	50	50	52	
Weapon stabilis-ation:	no	yes + commander's cupola	yes	yes	yes	yes	yes	yes	no	no, com-mander's cupola	Pz61 no Pz68 yes	yes
Rangefinder:	yes	Laser	Laser	Laser	Mk 1-4 spotting MG Mk 5 Laser	Laser	Stereo-scopic (AS1 and C1 Laser)	Laser	yes	yes	yes	Laser
Night sight:	IR driving	IR firing	Thermal night sight and passive driving	IR firing and passive driving	IR firing passive driving	As Mk 5	Thermal night sight and passive driving	Passive	IR firing passive driving	IR firing passive driving	No	No

B Numbers of Vehicles

USA	10,000	USSR	41,500
NATO (and France)	13,000	Warsaw Pact	16,000
Total	23,000	Countries outside Warsaw Pact	23,000
		Total	80,500

Type:	T54/55	T62	T72
Country:	USSR	USSR	USSR
Combat weight: (tons)	36.5	38	40
Power to weight ration (kW/ton (hp/ton))	10.5 (14.3)	13.7 (18.6)	18.4 (25)
Maximum speed: (km/h)	48	50	70
Radius: (km)	630 with expendable fuel tanks	350 without expendable fuel tanks	500
Main gun calibre: (mm)	100	115 (smoothbore)	125 (smoothbore)
No of rounds:	34 (T54) 43 (T55) 40 (T59)	40 (12 APDS-FS, m/v 1,640m/sec sub-calibre KE projectile) 7 HEAT-FS, m/v 1,000m/sec 21 HE-FS, m/v 800m/sec)	32, including 28 in the loader
Weapon stabilisation:	yes; elevation only	yes; elevation and azimuth	yes; elevation and azimuth
Rangefinder:	Scale; Reticle	Scale; Reticle	Laser
Night sight:	IR-firing, -driving	IR-firing, -driving	Passive

2. Contractors involved in the production of Leopard

Approximately 2,700 firms are involved in the production of components for the Leopard MBT; some 450 of them are direct sub-contractors to the General Contractor, Krauss-Maffei AG of Munich. Only the more important of these subcontractors are listed in the following paragraphs.

Rheinmetall Gmbh of Düsseldorf

Rheinmetall is a familiar name in the armament field. This firm produces the weapon system – other than the tube – for Leopard 1 and assembles part of the turrets. It also manufactures the commander's hatches, loader's hatches and AA machine gun mountings. Its most recent development has been the 120mm smoothbore gun for Leopard 2.

Together with the Kassel firm of Wegmann, Rheinmetall is undertaking the production and final assembly of the turret for Leopard 2.

Blohm & Voss AG of Hamburg

Well-known in the German ship-building industry and a member of the Thyssen group, Blohm & Voss have extensive experience and are experts in the welding and mechanical treatment of armour steel. Apart from hulls and welded turrets for the Leopard, this firm also produces turrets for the Marder APC, and the turret casings and hulls for the AA tank Gepard.

Waggonfabrik und Fahrzeugbau Wegmann & Co, of Kassel

Like Rheinmetall, Wegmann is an old established firm. (In World War 1 Wegmann built tanks, and in World War 2, the firm supplied turrets for Panzers I, II, III and the Tiger.) Together with Rheinmetall Wegmann produces turrets for the Leopard 1 and Leopard 2, and for the AA tank Gepard. Additionally Wegmann produces a whole series of components such as electrical equipment and smoke launching systems. Wegmann is also participating in studies for the turret of the next generation of tanks to follow Leopard 2.

Moreover Wegmann is more than a mere manufacturer of components. Systems for the Gepard turret are put together and tested at a facility specially equipped for this purpose. A Gepard turret is composed of roughly 50 components with more than 10,000 individual parts. A computer controlled test system checks out the turret system in only a few hours, a task which would require three men to work approximately seven weeks using conventional test methods.

Maschinenbau GmbH of Kiel (MaK)

MaK, a member of the Krupp Group, together with Porsche and Jung developed the Leopard 1. After the main contract was awarded to Krauss-Maffei MaK was subsequently made general contractor for the armoured recovery, armoured engineer and armoured birdgelayer vehicles. This firm also handles 50% of the machining work on the Leopard hulls and produces the electrical stowage boxes and cabling for the chassis. Currently MaK is developing a prototype for the new Combat Engineer Vehicle (GPM).

Moteren- und Turbinen Union Friedrichshafen GmbH
MTU manufactures the MB838 CaM-500 diesel engine for the Leopard which was designed and developed by Daimler Benz AG. (Daimler-Benz has no contractual commitments to the series production of armoured vehicles – and apparently does not want any.)

Friedrich Boysen GmbH, Altensteig, Black Forest
This firm which specialises in the muffling of internal combustion engines developed and supplies the Leopard's exhaust system.

Clouth Gummiwerke of Cologne
This firm vulcanises the rubber tyres on the roadwheel and support roller rims. Clouth was also involved in the development of the steel-reinforced armour skirts.

Deugra GmbH of Ratingen
Deugra, a subsidiary of the UK firm of Graviner, supplies the automatic fire extinguishing system of the Leopard.

DIEHL KG of Remscheid
Diehl is the leading track manufacturer in the Federal Republic. The company is now producing the tracks for the production vehicles.

Drägerwerk of Lübeck and Naton Piller KG of Osterode
These two firms are together producing the ventilation and NBC protection system jointly developed by them.

J. Eberspächer KG Esslingen, Neckar
This firm supplies the water preheating and air heating equipment.

Elektro Spezial GmbH of Bremen
A company of the Philips corporation, which supplies the image intensified driver's periscope for night driving.

Eltro GmbH & Company, Gesellschaft für Strahlungstechnik of Heidelberg
Produces the infra-red sight which can be substituted for the day panoramic telescope when the vehicle is to be operated at night.

Otto Fuchs, Metallwerke, Meinerzhagen (Bergisches Land)
Produce various aluminium extruded and forged parts for the Leopard.

Feinmechanische Werke Mainz GmbH
Their partner companies are Cadillac Gauge Company Detroit, Luther-Werke Braunschweig and AEG-Telefunken. They are supplying the turret control and weapon stabilisation system.

Hermann Hemscheid, Maschinenfabrik, Wuppertal
Manufactures shock absorbers for the Leopard suspension system.

Luther-Werke of Braunschweig
This firm participated in the development of the Leopard chassis and supplies components for the chassis of the series production.

Standard Elektrik Lorenz AG Stuttgart (SEL)
SEL, a subsidiary of International Telephone and Telegraph Corporation of New York, produces the Leopard's intercom system.

Steinheil – Lear Siegler AG, Ismaning
Supplies the commander's panoramic telescope and associated electrical equipment.

Süddeutsche Kühlerfabrik Julius Fr. Behr, Stuttgart
Supplies the Leopard's cooling system, coolant, coolers for the transmission oil cooling and the preheating element installed in the engine's oil reservoir.

Alfred Teves GmbH, Frankfurt/Main
Supplies the Leopard's hydraulic brake system.

VAW Leichtmetal-Werke Bonn
Supplies roadwheel and turret race ring components, fuel tanks and ammunition brackets.

Zahnradfabrik Friedrichshafen AG
Manufactures the combined hydraulic planetary steer-shift transmission and the final drives for the Leopard.

Carl Zeiss, Oberkochen
Produces the range finder and telescope for the Leopard's optical fire control system.

Hoesch Rote Erde – Schmiededag AG Dortmund
Supplies the Leopard turret race ring and drive sprockets for the tracks.

Arnold Jung, Lokomotivfabrik GmbH, Jungenthal/ Kirchen/Sieg
Jung-Jungenthal in conjunction with Luther, MaK and Porsche helped in the development of the prototype of the Leopard, and subsequently the prototypes of the armoured recovery vehicle. For the Leopard series production the firm supplies suspension units, track parts, and hulls recovery equipment and steering units.

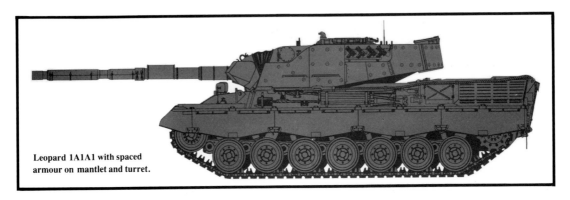

Leopard 1A1A1 with spaced
armour on mantlet and turret.

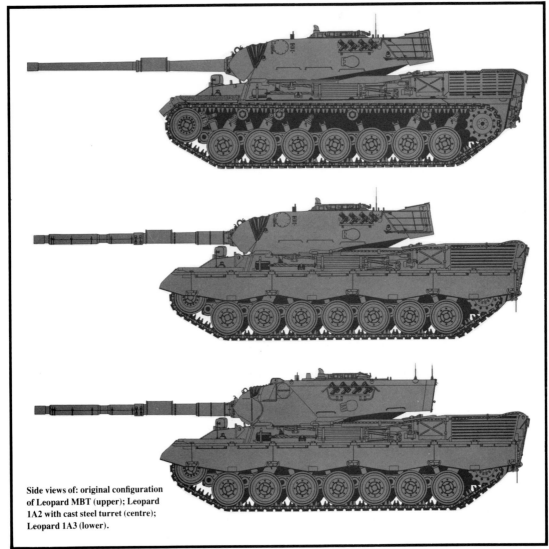

Side views of: original configuration
of Leopard MBT (upper); Leopard
1A2 with cast steel turret (centre);
Leopard 1A3 (lower).

3. Specifications

BATTLE TANK INDIA PROJECT '714'

Country of manufacture: India
Manufacturer: Porsche System Engineering Ltd and Daimler-Benz AG (design)
Year of manufacture: Planned 1954/55. None built.
Crew: Four (commander, gunner, loader/operator, driver)
Armament: *Main* One 90mm main gun, 61 rounds carried
Secondary Two MGs, 4,000 rounds carried
Armour: *Hull* 90mm front, 60-90mm sides, 45mm back
Turret 90-130mm front, 45-90mm sides, 45mm back
Engine: Daimler-Benz 29.9litre MB837A water-cooled diesel; eight-cylinder 90° (165mm bore, 175 stroke) compression ration 18.2:1
Fuel: Pump system; 160litre/100km consumption; 120litre (26.37gal)
Transmission: Three-disc clutch; five forward and five reverse gears; rear drive
Suspension: Springs
Brakes: Daimler-Benz/Porsche mechanical disc
Wheels: Support rollers (road wheels)
Max speed: 50km/h (30mph)
Range: 450km
Width: 3.2m overall
Length: 6.2m overall
10.2m with gun
4.38m track on ground
Height: 2.8m
Weight: 39,500kg (max)
28,650kg chassis
10,850kg turret
1,680kg payload
Ground pressure: 0.74kg/sq cm
Turning circle: On own axis
Max gradient: 60%
Fording depth: 1.4m (max)
Ditch crossing: 2.7m (max)

STANDARD PANZER PROTOTYPE A-1 '723'
(italic figures in brackets show Prototype A-2 differences)

Country of manufacture: Germany
Manufacturer: Arn Jung Lokomotivenfabrik GmbH
Year of manufacture: Two built 1960-61 *(62)*
Crew: Four
Armament: *Main* One 105mm L7A1 *(L7A3)*, 58 *(60)* rounds carried
Secondary One MG42 *(MG3)*, 3,000 rounds carried
Armour: *Hull* 50mm *(70mm)* front, 30mm *(30-35mm)* sides, 20mm *(25mm)* back
Turret 60mm all round
Engine: As for Project '714' *(Daimler-Benz 37.33litre MB838 Ca-500 10-cylinder)*
Fuel: As for Project '714'; capacity 1,120litre *(1,010litre)* in three containers
Transmission: As for Project '714' *(ZF4 HP-250 Hydromedia, hydraulic torque converter clutch; four forward and two reverse gears)*
Suspension: Torsion bars, transverse
Brakes: A. Teves automatic disc *(A. Teves hydraulic servo disc)*
Wheels: Support (road wheels) and idling rollers
Max speed: 61.3km/h *(65km/h)*
Range: 550km *(470km)*
Width: 3.15m *(3.25m)* overall
Length: 8.01m *(8.07m)*
9.38m *(9.12m)* with gun
4.11m *(4.16m)* track on ground
Height: 2.2m *(2.29m)*
Ground clearance: 0.4m *(0.45m)*
Weight: 33,300kg *(38,500kg)* max
25,000kg *(30,000kg)* chassis
c8,000kg *(c9,000kg)* turret
2,840kg *(2,780kg)* payload
Ground pressure: 0.8kg/sq cm *(0.84kg/sq cm)*
Turning circle: On own axis *(10.2m as well)*
Max gradient: 60%
Max vertical object: 1.1m
Fording depth. 1.23m *(1.19m)*
Ditch crossing: 3.0m

STANDARDPANZER PROTOTYPE B-1 Type T-I

(italic figures in brackets indicate B-2 Type T-II differences)

Country of manufacture: Germany
Manufacturer: Rheinstahl Hanomag AG, Hannover Works *(Herschel Werke AG, Kassel)*
Year of manufacture: Two build 1960-61 *(1962; six vehicles ordered but only two produced; one by Hanomag)*
Crew: Four
Armament: *Main* One 105mm semi-automatic *(BK L7A2)*, 63 rounds carried
Secondary Two MG3s, 2,400 *(5,000)* rounds carried
Armour: *Hull* 50mm *(70mm)* front, 25mm *(30mm)* sides, 15mm *(25mm)* back
Turret 60mm all round
Engine: As for Project '714' *(Daimler-Benz 37.33litre MB838 Ca-500 10-cylinder)*
Fuel: As for Project '714'; capacity 420litre *(820litre)*
Transmission: Pub PP45 *(PP45 II)* lamellae clutch; five *(eight)* forward and five *(eight)* reverse gears; rear drive

Suspension: B1 Hydrop (Frieste and Höpfner) *(conventional spring, one with torsion bar)*
Brakes: B1 Hydraulic *(servo-hydraulic)* disc
Wheels: Road and idling *(support and idling rollers)*
Max speed: 63km/h *(65km/h)*
Range: 200km *(300km)*
Width: 3.15m *(3.25m)* overall
Length: 7.84m *(8.27m)*
9.4m *(9.44m)* with gun
3.8m *(4.02m)* track on ground
Height: 2.12m *(2.31m)*
Ground clearance: 0.4m
Weight: 35,800kg *(38,980kg)* max
26,660kg *(29,170kg)* chassis
8,735kg *(9,370kg)* turret
2,320kg *(2,670kg)* payload
Ground pressure: 0.957kg/sq cm *(0.84kg/sq cm)*
Turning circle: 9.7m *(2.6m)*
Max gradient: 60%
Climbing ability: 0.8m *(0.95m)*
Fording depth: 1.2-2.1m
Ditch crossing: 2.8m

LEOPARD PRODUCTION VARIANTS

Manufacturer: Krauss-Maffei AG
Number produced:
1,845 (Leopard 1 first, second, third and fourth batches redesignated 1A1)
232 (1A2)
110 (1A3)
250 (1A4)
Crew: Four
Armament: *Main* One 105mm BK L7A3 (L/51), 60 rounds carried
Secondary Two MG3s, 5,500 rounds carried (3,000 Leopard 1 1st/2nd batches)
Armour: *Hull* 70mm front, 25-35mm sides, 25mm back
Turret 60mm
Engine: Motoren- und Turbinen Union (MTU) 37.33litre MB838 Ca-M500 water-cooled diesel; 10-cylinder (165mm stroke, 175mm bore) compression ratio 19.5:1 developing 830hp at 2,200 rpm
Fuel: Pump system; 165litre/100km (185litre Leopard 1s); capacity 985litre in two containers (1,010litre Leopard 1 1st/2nd batches)
Transmission: ZF 4HP-250, four forward and two reverse gears, rear drive
Suspension: Torsion bars, transverse
Brakes: A. Teves hydraulic-servo disc
Wheels: Support and idling rollers
Max road speed: 65km/h /64km/h Leopard 1 1st/2nd batches)

Road range: 600km (550km Leopard 1 1st/2nd batches)
Width: 3.25m (without skirts)
3.37m (1A4 with skirts)
Length: 6.94m
9.54m with gun forwards
4.24 track on ground
Height: 2.62m
2.76m (1A4)
Ground clearance: 0.44m (9.45m Leopard 1 1st/2nd batches)
Max weight: 39,600kg (Leopard 1 1st/2nd batches)
40,000kg (Leopard 1 3rd batch)
41,500kg (1A1)
42,500kg (1A2, 1A3, 1A4)
Chassis weight: 32,000kg (31,000kg Leopard 1 all batches)
Max payload: 2,000kg
Ground pressure: 0.84kg/sq cm (Leopard 1 1st/2nd batches)
0.86kg/sq cm (Leopard 1 3rd batch)
0.88kg/sq cm /1A1, 1A4)
0.90kg/sq cm /1A2, 1A3)
Turning circle: 9.6m (10.2m and own axis for Leopard 1 1st/2nd batches)
Max gradient: 60%
Climbing ability: 1.1m
Fording depth: 2.2/4.0m
Ditch crossing: 2.9m

ARMOURED RECOVERY VEHICLE
(italic figures in brackets show prototype differences from production model)

Country of Manufacture: Germany
Manufacturer: Atlas-MAK Maschinenbau GmbH Kiel
(Arn Jung Lokomotivenfabrik GmbH)
Year of manufacture: 1966-71 *(1964)*
Number built: 444 *(2)*
Crew: Four
Armament: Two MG3s, 3,000 rounds carried
Armour: 35mm front, 25-30mm sides, 25mm back
Engine: As for Leopard MBT *(Daimler-Benz MB838 Ca-500, compression ratio 18.2:1)*
Fuel: Pump system; 245litre/100km *(200-400litre/100km);* capacity 1,550litre in two containers

Transmission, Suspension, Brakes, Wheels: As for Leopard MBT
Max speed: 62km/h *(65km/h)*
Range: 500km *(840km)*
Width: 3.25m
Length: 7.45m *(7.16m)*
4.24m *(4.22m)* track on ground
Height: 2.7m *(2.2m)*
Ground clearance: 0.44m *(0.45m)*
Max weight: 39,800kg *(40,000kg)*
600kg payload
Ground pressure: 0.85kg/sq cm *(0.86kg/sq cm)*
Turning circle: 3.65m *(10.2m and on own axis)*
Max gradient: 60%
Vertical obstacle: 1.15m *(1.1m)*
Fording depth: 2.1/4m *(1.2/4m)*
Ditch crossing: 2.9m

ARMOURED ENGINEER VEHICLE

Manufacturer: Atlas-MAK Maschinenbau GmbH, Kiel
Year of manufacture: 1968-71
Number built: 105
Crew: Four
Armament: Two MG3s, 3,000 rounds carried
Armour: 35mm front, 25-30mm sides, 25mm back
Engine: As for Leopard MBT
Fuel: Pump system; 245litre/100km; capacity 1,550litre in two containers
Transmission: As for Leopard MBT but four reverse gears
Suspension, Brakes, Wheels: As for Leopard MBT
Max speed: 62km/h

Range: 800km
Width: 3.25m
Length: 7.88m
4.24m track on ground
Height: 2.7m
Ground clearance: 0.44m
Max weight: 40,800kg
600kg payload
Ground pressure: 0.87kg/sq cm
Turning circle: 10.2m or on own axis
Max gradient: 60%
Verticle obstacle: 1.0m
Fording depth: 2.1/4.0m
Ditch crossing: 2.9m

ARMOURED BRIDGELAYER BIBER

Manufacturer: Atlas-MAK Maschinenbau GmbH, Kiel
Year of manufacture: 1973-75
Number built: 105
Crew: Four
Armament: None
Armour: 70mm front, 35mm sides, 25mm back
Engine: As for Leopard MBT
Fuel: Pump system; 180litre/100km; capacity 1,010litre in two containers
Transmission, Suspension, Brakes, Wheels: As for Leopard MBT
Max speed: 62km/h
Range: 800km
Width: 3.25mm
4.0m with bridge

4m bridge
Length: 10.2m
11.4 with bridge
4.24m track on ground
22m bridge
Height: 2.56m
3.5m with bridge
Ground clearance: 0.44m
Weight: 35,000kg max
45,000kg with bridge
Ground pressure: 0.96kg/sq cm
Turning circle: 10.2m
Max gradient: 60%
Verticle obstacle: 1.0m
Fording depth: 1.2/1.7m
Ditch crossing: 3.0m

ANTI-AIRCRAFT TANK GEPARD

Manufacturer: Krauss-Maffei AG
Year of manufacture: 1974-6
Number built: Production figure not yet known.
Crew: Three
Armament: two 35mm MK Oerlikon cannon
Armour: 70mm front, 35mm sides, 25mm back
Engine: As for Leopard MBT
Fuel: Pump system; 180litre/100km; capacity 1,010litre in two containers
Transmission, Suspension, Brakes, Wheels and Max speed: As for Leopard MBT
Range: 550km
Width: 3.25m
Length: 7.28m
4.24m track on ground
Height: 3.01m
Ground clearance: 0.44m
Weight: 45,600kg max
30,600kg chassis
14,000kg turret
1,300kg payload (1,100kg ammunition)
Ground pressure: 0.95kg/sq cm
Turning circle: 10.2m
Max gradient: 60%
Vertical obstacle: 1.12m
Fording depth: 1.2/4.0m
Ditch crossing: 3.0m

Gepard Fire Control System
Search radar
Contractor: Siemens AG, Munich
Operating frequency: S-Band
Range: 15km
Fixed echo suppression: Pulse doppler principle at approx 60dB magnitude
Antenna rotation speed: 60rpm
Integrated IFF: Yes

Tracking radar
Contractor: Siemens-Albis AG, Zürich

Operating frequency: Ku-Band
Range: 15km
Fixed echo suppression: Pulse doppler principle at 23dB magnitude

Fire control computer
Contractor: Contraves AG, Zürich
Operating principle: Miniaturised analog computer
Target speed range: 0 – approx Mach 1.5
Corrections: automatic Muzzle Velocity V_0, Cant manual (variables) – Wind direction, Ballistic air pressure, Ballistic temperature

Periscopic sight
Contractor: Contraves AG, Züich; Fisba AG, St Gallen
Type: monocular
Magnification: ×1.5/6
Field of view: 50°/12.5°
Training limits: In azimuth – 360°
In elevation –10° to +85°

Guns
Contractor: Werkzeugmaschinenfabrik Oerlikon-Bührle AG, Zürich
Type: Automatic gun with gas operated breech
Calibre: 35mm
Barrel length: L90 = 3.15m
Rate of fire/gun: 550rounds/min
Muzzle velocity V_0: 1,175m/sec
Elevation limits: —5° to +85°

Ammunition feed
Type: Hydraulic operated belt feed
Ammunition carried; AA – 640 rounds
Surface target – 40 rounds

Ammunition
Type: AA – HE
Surface target – APDS, anti-tank
Weight of round: 1,560g
Weight of projectile: 550g
Flight time: Over 1,000m – 0.95sec
Over 3,000m – 3.75sec

PANZERHAUBITZE GCT155 PROTOTYPE

Manufacturer: Krauss-Maffei AG and GIAT
Year of manufacture: 1973
Crew: Four
Armament: *Main* One 155mm GCT L/40 howitzer, 42 rounds carried with automatic loader
Secondary One 7.62mm MG, 2,000 rounds carried
Armour: *Hull* 35mm front, 30mm sides, 25mm back
Superstructure Thick enough to resist APDS rounds
Engine, Fuel, Transmission, Suspension, Brakes, Wheels, Max speed, Range, Width, Ground

clearance, Max gradient: As for Leopard MBT
Length: 7.09m
10.6m with gun forward
Height: 3.12m
Weight: 45,500kg
4,000kg payload
Ground pressure: 0.95kg/sq cm
Turning circle: 10.2m
Vertical obstacle: 1.2m
Fording depth: 2.25m
Ditch crossing: 2.9m

MBT-80 PROTOTYPE

Country of Manufacture: Germany/USA
Manufacturer: Deutsche Entwicklungs GmbH,
Augsburg
Year of manufacture: 1964-7
Crew: Three
Armament: One 152mm multi-purpose gun (USA)
One 120mm, one 20mm and one 7.62mm MG3 (German)
Armour: No details available
Engine: MTU MB873 Ka 39.8litre 10-cylinder (165mm
bore, 155mm stroke) compression ratio 20.5:1
Fuel: Pump system; 215litre/100km; capacity 1,320litre
Transmission: Renk HSWL 354, four forward and two
reverse gear, rear drive
Suspension: Hydropneumatic, height adjustable
Brakes: A. Teves hydraulic servo disc
Wheels: Support and idling rollers
Max speed: 70km/h

Range: 650km
Width: 3.51m
Length: 6.99m
9.1m with gun
4.65m track on ground
Height: 2.29m normal (1.99m lowered, 2.59 lifted)
Ground clearance: 0.44m normal (0.14m lowered,
0.74m lifted)
Weight: 46-50,000kg
29,000kg chassis
17,000kg turret
2,000kg payload
Ground pressure: 0.78kg/sq cm
Turning circle: 14m
Max gradient: 60%
Vertical obstacle: 1.1m
Fording depth: 2.25m
Ditch crossing: 2.8m

LEOPARD 2

Manufacturer: Krauss-Maffei AG
Crew: Four
Armament: *Main* One 120/105mm BK smoothbore
Secondary Two MGs
Armour: No details available
Engine: MTU MB873 Ka-500 39.8litre 12-cylinder
(165mm bore, 175mm stroke) compression ratio 20.5:1
developing 1,500hp at 2,600rpm
Fuel: Filling and drawing circle; 215litre/100km;
capacity 1,000litre
Transmission: Renk HSWL 354/3, four forward and two
reverse gears, rear drive
Suspension: Torsion bars, transverse
Brakes: A. Teves hydraulic servo disc

Wheels: Support and idling rollers
Max road speed: 68km/h
Road range: 500km
Width: 3.73m (with skirts)
Length: 7.4m (hull)
9.61m (gun forwards)
4.95m track on ground
Height: 2.48m
Ground clearance: 0.55 at front, 0.5m at back
Weight: 55,000kg max
Ground pressure: 0.85kg/sq cm
Turning circle: High axis
Max gradiant: 60%
Vertical obstacle: 1.12m
Fording depth: 2.2/5.5m
Ditch crossing: 3.2m

Bibliography

Books
For further reading the following books are
recommended:
Raimund Knecht (Ed); J. F. Lehmans Verlag Munich;
The Leopard Combat Tank; (originally published in 1972
in German as *Kampfpanzer Leopard)*
Walter J. Spielberger; *Der Mittlere Kampfpanzer
Leopard Und Seine Abarten;* Motorbuch Verlag,
Stuttgart.
Walter J. Spielberger; *Von der Zugmaschine zum
Leopard 2;* Bernard & Graefe Verlag, Munich.

Articles
A&W   *Armies & Weapons*
IWR   *Internationale Wehr-Revue*
JWT   *Jahrbuch der Wehrtechnik*
KT   *Kampftruppen*
MILTECH   *Military Technology*
SuT   *Soldat und Technik.*

On Leopard:
*Der Leopard, Deutsche Version des europaischen
Standardpanzers;* SuT8/63

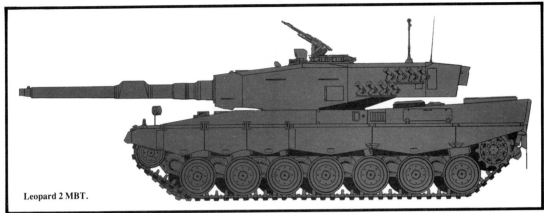

Leopard 2 MBT.

Chieftain und Leopard im Vergleich; SuT4/66
Der erste Leopard rollte vom Fliessband; SuT10/65
Dr. F. M. von Senger und Etterlin; Der Kampfpanzer
Leopard, Entwicklungsgeschichte und
Leistungsvergleich. SuT4/67
Der erste Leopard für Belgien; SuT/68
Leopard auch für Italien; SuT/70
KPz Leopard für Australien und Kanada;
Sonderausrüstungen; SuT3/77
Günther Müller; Stabilisierung der Waffenanlage des
Kampfpanzers; JWT 2
Theodor Icken, Heinrich Wüst; Panzerentwicklungen in
Ost und West; JWT 9
Leopard 1 System Maintenance; MilTech. 1/77
R. M. Ogorkiewicz; Panzersimulatoren; IWR 78
David Miller; Leopard Main Battle Tank; War Monthly
52/77
Christopher F. Foss; Krauss-Maffei. A study of the
Military Programmes; Defence 12/77
The Leopard with its mane; A&W 26/76
Leopard to the antipodes; A&W 43/78
H. D. von Bernuth, J. H. Reuter; Leopard – The German
Battle Tank; Armor 1/70
Dr F. M. von Senger und Etterlin; Operational Mobility –
A Function of Design. Leopard as a Noteworthy
Example; Armor 1/70
Oswald Filla; Waffenstabilisierungen in Kampfpanzern;
KT =/67
R. M. Ogorkiewicz; Production of the German Leopard
Tank; Automotive Industries 12/69

On the Recovery Vehicle and Armoured Engineer Vehicle

Theodor Icken; Prototyp des neuen deutschen
Bergepanzers. Erster Abkömmling der Panzerfamilie
Leopard; SuT8/64
Bergepanzer Leopard; KT5/66
Pionierpanzer Leopard; KT2/69
Bergepanzer Standard; Wehrkunde 15/66

On the Bridgelayer Biber

Brückenpanzer Leopard. Leopard-Fahrgestell mit zwei
Brückenversionen für Truppenversuch; SuT4/71
Brückenlegepanzer Biber an die Truppe übergeben.
Technische Entwicklung und gegenwärtiger Stand;
SuT2/74 S.64 SuT7/74
Hans Leue; Pionier-Brückengerät 1980, ein
Ideenwettbewerb; JWT 6
Engineer Vehicles; A&W33/77

On the AA Tank Gepard

Der Flakpanzer Leopard; SuT2/69
Norbert Roy; Der neue Flakpanzer der Bundeswehr;
SuT8/72
Walter J. Spielberger; Weapon System Monograph:
Gepard Anti-Aircraft Tank; MILTECH 4/78
Gepard; A&W27/76
Enrico Po; Oerlikon 35-mm; A&W15/75
Christopher F. Foss; Self-Propelled Anti-Aircraft AFVs;
Battle 4/75

On the Leopard 2

Leopard 2 Program; MILTECH1/77
The 120mm-Smooth Bore Gun System for the Main
Battle Tank; MILTECH 1/77
Leopard 2 in the USA. A German Point of View;
MILTECH 2/77
Leopard 2 AV – Der zukünftige Standardpanzer der
NATO?; IWR 78
Robert Heck; Leopard 2 – Deutschlands Kampfpanzer für
die 80er Jahre; Armada 2/78
Enrico Po; Leopard 2; A&W23/76
G. M. Bailly-Cowell; MBT Leopard 2 AV for NATO?;
NATO's Fifteen Nations 3/76
Main Battle Tank Leopard 2 for the German Army;
NATO's Fifteen Nations 5/77
R. M. Ogorkiewicz; Leopard 2AV; Armor 1/78
W. John Farquharson; Leopard 2 – NATO's Next Tank;
Armed Forces Journal 12/75